Restoring
OUR REPUBLIC

*The Making of the Republic and How
We Reclaim It Before It's Too Late*

NED RYUN

Praise for
RESTORING OUR REPUBLIC

"*Restoring Our Republic* is powerful love letter to the United States of America. Detailed and sweeping, yet digestible and engrossing, this is the book America needs right now, a potent antidote to the poisonous lies promulgated by today's elite, those unworthy heirs of the exponential greater men of the founding. Ned Ryun gives us back our history, and in doing so reveals the truth about who we are as Americans."

— Kurt Schlichter, Senior Columnist at Townhall.com

"Ned Ryun nails it with *Restoring Our Republic*. Our Founder Fathers weren't anarchic revolutionaries. They fought instead to preserve our Judeo-Christian Civilization. That civilization, the greatest ever, is under lethal assault once more from those who detest President Trump's MAGA agenda. Read *Restoring Our Republic* to refuel your commitment and help win back our country."

— Sebastian Gorka Ph.D. Former Strategist to President Donald Trump, Host of America First

"The success of our republic isn't by chance: it is due to disciplined, deliberate choices. The growth of socialism now threatens the freedom this success provides. How will Americans now choose? Ned Ryun's *Restoring Our Republic* examines this and celebrates the DNA of American liberty."

— Dana Loesch, nationally syndicated radio host and best-selling author

"*Restoring Our Republic* is both a love letter and a call to arms. As the republic of liberty created by the settlers of this country is slowly replaced with a new regime, Ryun reminds us of what we had and how we can get it back. This is not simply a diagnostic, much less a eulogy, it is a plan for the reinvigoration of our nation, for the unity of her people, and for the restoration of the Republic."
 — **Chris Buskirk, Publisher and Editor of American Greatness**

"Ned Ryun incisively details the fundamental principles and history of freedom and liberty that made America great, as well as the disastrous consequences of throwing overboard the constitutional ideals of the Founding Fathers. *Restoring Our Republic* makes clear that the only way to make America great again is to keep America free."
 — **Sean Davis, co-founder of The Federalist**

"Ned Ryun's *Restoring Our Republic* is a great analysis of what we've fought for, where we've been, and where we're going."
 — **Dan Bongino, The Dan Bongino Show**

"*Restoring Our Republic* is a historical road map of how the United States of America came to be the greatest force for good the world has ever known. Ned Ryun explains the complex underpinnings of the American experiment and pulls no punches in warning of the fragility of American exceptionalism. Understanding that America's constitutional and legal foundation was laid thousands, not hundreds of years ago, Ned calls on Americans to appreciate the gift they've been given, while warning of the dangers ahead if they stray from the Founders' course. A celebration of western civilization and values, *Restoring Our Republic* reminds us that a strong America means a return to our core tenets. This book is sure to become the must read manifesto of Constitutional conservatives."
 — **John Cardillo, Host of America Talks Live**

DEDICATION

◆

For Becca, Nathaniel, James, Charlotte, and Hudson.
You mean the world to me and have made "home" such a beautiful word:
no matter where I am in the world I know I'm coming home to you.

Exegi monumentum aere perennius
regalique situ pyramidum altius,
quod non imber edax, non Aquilo impotens
possit diruere…

Horace, 23 BC

RESTORING OUR REPUBLIC

First edition published 2019.
Printed in the United States of America

ISBN: 9781705870778

CONTENTS

AUTHOR'S NOTE

◆

It's my hope that those reading this book will come away with a greater understanding, and of course, appreciation for what we as Americans have been given. In the midst of great prosperity and freedom it is human nature to take such things for granted. But we have flourished as a nation for a reason. It is not chance that we have achieved all that we have in a relatively short amount of time. As history shows us, however, apathy and lack of knowledge sow the seeds of demise. In the face of aggressive socialism, ignorance and quite frankly a far Left in America inspired and driven by deeply un-American ideology, the question is what will our response actually be? Do we even know what we are fighting for? It says in the Bible that a people perish for lack of knowledge; they perish for many reasons, but if there is no knowledge, there can be no intellectual defense, no way to first mitigate and stop, and then proactively dismantle a destructive ideology.

I would never make any claims that this book is an all-encompassing one; it was never intended to be. But I do hope that after reading this book you will be inspired to fight for this republic. It has been a "name and a praise" for untold millions who have experienced freedom and prosperity because of it and it continues to serve as that great beacon of hope to freedom loving people around the world. It can continue to be that *if* we will determine to fight for it: let us seek to defend and renew what we have been given, but even more so, let us seek a golden age for this country in which we climb to even greater heights of freedom and prosperity.

Keep America Free.

Ned Ryun
Elysium Farm
Fall 2019

CHAPTER ONE

Greatness is a Choice

———— ◆ ————

It is hard to overstate the impact the United States has had on the world since the original 13 colonies declared independence from Great Britain in the summer of 1776. From a small, primarily agrarian nation on the edge of a Eurocentric world, it rose to become the world's superpower, the center of the global economy.

Our American republic is a singular nation, the likes of which has never before been seen. History has seen and experienced aspects of this republic, from the time of the ancient Hebrews and Greeks, to the Romans and the English. The sum of traditions, practices, and beliefs drawn from those civilizations, the lessons learned, all informed what this nation would become. These various threads of the rule of law and separation of powers and the proper relation between the state and man were all drawn together to form the fabric of a new society and nation. But there has never been a nation like this republic in the history of the world.

Founded on individual liberty and voluntary association, this country has had its share of sins, with slavery being one of the most egregious. But that should not surprise us given our imperfect world filled with imperfect human beings. Even more so, we should expect a government, no matter how well intended its principles and values, to be imperfect when it is filled with imperfect human beings.

Yet despite all of its faults, these United States have become the envy of the world, providing the greatest amount of freedom and opportunity to the greatest number of people, more than any other nation throughout history. Its status in the world, its exceptionalism, its freedom, its opportunities, are not the products of chance. They did not just happen. They are the result of very intentional and distinct decisions made centuries ago.

Consider that in the age of the divine right of kings, our young republic set another course: there would be no king, no powers concentrated in the hands of the few, no belief that the king was the law. The law would be king in this new nation. It would be a government of, by, and for the people, not people for the government, nor man for the state. Now with this republic, the state was to be for the man: an advocate, defender, guardian, and steward of all the natural rights of the people as given to them by their Creator.

The men who founded this republic were optimistic realists. They were deeply realistic about human nature with its multitude of flaws and shortcomings, yet they were optimistic that they could in fact, working with imperfect human nature, create a government that protected all of the God-given rights to life, liberty, and the pursuit of happiness. Faced with the challenge of protecting and advancing these rights while creating a government strong enough to defend those rights from both foreign and domestic threats, the Founders infused the nascent republic with transcendent values that would stand the test of time. It is not hyperbole to assert that the United States Constitution is one of the greatest, if not *the* greatest, political documents of all time.

Yet in the centuries that have passed since our founding, we have drifted from those principles, intentionally, and sadly, through ignorance as well. Many know that these principles exist, and we can see vestiges of them, yet, as Yeats writes, we seem to drift in ever-widening gyres from our beginnings; the "falcon does not hear the falconer." Worse yet, it seems now that the best truly do "lack all conviction while the worst are filled with passionate intensity."[1]

This great drifting began in earnest at the dawn of the 20th century with the rise of the Progressives, whose beliefs about human nature and the role of government and power differed greatly from those of the Founders. The Progressives, who were both Democrats and Republicans, armed with all the fervor of religious zealots, determined that science and an educated elite would accelerate human progress. Frustrated by the Founders' Constitution that limited government and separated powers, the Progressives set forth on a great expansion of the state, sure that a powerful Administrative State would solve society's ills. In their minds, the state was not a necessary evil against which the American people defended their

---

1   W.B. Yeats, *The Second Coming*, https://poets.org/poem/second-coming as accessed September 20, 2019.

rights, but was now the *provider* from which the American people could *claim* their rights.

Whereas the Founders were optimistic realists, the Progressives were utopian statists, deeply naive about human nature and the dangers of concentrated power. They mistakenly sought utopia in a fallen world, then compounded that mistake by concentrating tremendous power in the hands of a relatively few, deeply imperfect, human beings. In their minds, human nature was not inherently evil but was perfectable. Unelected, educated elites were to fill the envisioned Administrative State, separated from politics and elected officials and the accountability the people's representatives bring, as much as possible. The walls separating the powers of government were knocked down and power consolidated to advance progress.

In rapid succession, the Progressives would pass four Constitutional amendments between 1912 and 1920 (the 16th, 17th, 18th, and 19th), while launching the Federal Reserve, the Federal Trade Commission, and numerous other agencies and government initiatives. It was a triumph of statism, the quaint notions of limited government and separation of powers nothing but tired old ideas propounded by wig-wearing, benighted men of the 18th century. "We are not bound to adhere to the doctrines held by the signers of the Declaration of Independence; we are as free as they were to make and unmake governments. We are not here to worship men or a document," Woodrow Wilson declared.[2]

---

2   Woodrow Wilson, *"The Author and Signers of the Declaration of Independence,"* in Pestritto, Wilson: Essential Political Writings, pp. 97-105.

The first wave of Progressives would eventually give rise to a second, with Franklin Roosevelt, and then a third, with Lyndon Johnson. By the 200th anniversary of the birth of the republic, the Founders would have found the government the Progressives formed far different than what they (the Founders) had envisioned. The state had displaced the individual as the central focus of the nation. The size of government, but more importantly, the *scope* of government, was now invasive and overbearing, far above and beyond the powers the Founders had ever deemed possible, or desirable, for a people to remain free.

From a government that originally started with three departments in 1789: State, Treasury, and the War Department, the federal bureaucracy has grown to the unimaginable size of more than 430 departments, agencies, and sub-agencies, populated with millions of government employees. This self-replicating Administrative State was, and is, the realization of Progressive dreams: a massive bureaucracy filled with millions of unelected bureaucrats, all attempting to address and regulate as much of American life as possible. This Administrative State is filled with reinforcing loops, the idea that something once started, never stops, and only grows, and it strengthens itself internally year after year. This sprawling, invasive, inefficient state is the foundation for and has given rise to what is today referred to as the **Swamp** of Washington, DC.

Washington now has a whiff of Versailles[3] about it, run by a ruling class of both parties that are detached from, and filled with, great disdain for the mere "peasants," the "irredeemable deplorables" in the outer world. This ruling class, bolstered and funded by its cronies and special interests, has rigged the system of government to serve its own interests, not those of the American people. Even more troubling, the unelected bureaucrats, *funded* by the people, placed in power to supposedly *serve* the people, now consider themselves *above* the people. Elections are merely dates on a calendar that are quaint notions of a representative republic, celebrations of a relic of government that no longer truly exists. Elections come and go, but the Administrative State and those who fill it remain.

This Ruling Class and Administrative State now *run* a system of government far removed from the people, but even more importantly, not working on behalf of the people. It works *against* the people, taxing them at levels far above and beyond what our Founders would have ever imagined, putting the weight of an incredibly heavy regulatory state on the shoulders of the American people, striking trade deals and implementing foreign policy that sell out the interests of Americans every day.

In the Swamp, the rule of law is more a series of suggestions in which only certain people are guilty, while others, depending

---

3   During the time of Louis XVI, the wealthy and the well-connected enjoyed immense privilege while the vast majority of French society, including many who understood basic political and civil rights, did not. The system, manipulated by the king and the nobility, assured their wealth and comfort at the expense of everyone else, all while residing in the seat of power, Versailles, far away and detached from the everyday needs and priorities of society. Versailles and modern Washington DC have more in common than the elites would care to admit.

on their political connections or wealth, are allowed to walk free, no matter how flagrant their behavior. The bifurcated legal system is now more a weapon to be used against political opponents over policy differences; the equal application of the law a farce.

Today, elected officials can operate in Washington, DC, bolstered and protected by collaborators in the media industry, and discuss coercive socialism as though such ideas were perfectly normal instead of the destructive ones they truly are. In this world detached from reality, people can openly propose, and defend, infanticide and not be ostracized from society. The idea that government is to protect the basic rights of life, liberty, property, and the pursuit of happiness, *and take none of them away*, is an idea best left to the pages of old history books. The ideas of natural rights, the true purpose of government to protect persons and property, and just and voluntary associations are ideas that are ignored and dismissed.

Yet civilizations and societies come apart at the seams when there is no rule of law, no respect for human life and human dignity and property. When society no longer understands and embraces these principles, then all that a people are left with are competing opinions based on emotion and the latest thought they read on social media. But society cannot stand that tension for long: people desire peace and prosperity, and the tension must be resolved. Opinions must compete with other opinions, might becomes the determiner of right, and one set of opinions must win out. Those opinions must become the new value proposition for a nation, and those who do not agree will be compelled, by force, to accept the new standards of truth.

But this does not have to be.

We were founded upon transcendent truths: truths that stand outside the changing whims of men and women, truths that are immovable and that stand the test of time. These truths comprise the rule of law, individual rights, and voluntary association, and they are the essence of Western Civilization. They made us the greatest nation the world has ever seen. But now, the important questions are: "Can we return to our founding principles? Can there be a reformation and a renewal?" The answer to both: "Not unless people know where we've come from, because to *not* know our past is to be blind." We cannot know where we are to go unless we know from where we came. It is only in understanding the past and these values that we can once again renew our republic.

CHAPTER TWO
The Republic's Great Traditions

———— ◆ ————

Americans today—without realizing it—are enjoying the great legacy of Western Civilization. The understanding and practice of human dignity and freedom were developed, refined, and passed down to us over millennia, from the Hebrews to the Greeks and Romans, to the English and to the American Founders to the present day. In many ways, America is the culminating expression of Western thought. The "idea" that was—and is—America has provided untold numbers of people a level of freedom and prosperity unprecedented in human history.

Today some seem to know instinctively that we want to preserve and emulate these "principles" of Western Civilization that were passed down to us via our Founding Fathers. But why? What do we see in our Founders and in their principles that is so worthy of emulation? Do we really cherish these principles, or do we simply not want to lose the prosperity we have so long enjoyed? To appreciate them, we have to first understand the transcendent principles that inspired our Founders.

It is important to understand that the American Revolution was not a "revolution" as we understand the term today. The Founding Fathers were not radicals seeking to overthrow an establishment—they would have been the first to deny such a claim. Instead, they strove to preserve age-old customs and to defend liberties that they believed to be theirs by right and inheritance. Theirs was more of a restoration, a return, to their inherent God-given natural rights and liberties. They didn't draw their principles out of thin air—rather, they sought to affirm and even institutionalize precepts already deeply rooted within the culture.

Alexis de Tocqueville, a young Frenchman who visited and studied America in the early 19th century, picked up on this non-revolutionary aspect of the American Revolution. "The revolution in the United States was produced by a mature and reflective taste for freedom," he wrote, "and not by a vague and indefinite instinct of independence. It was not supported by passions of disorder; but, on the contrary, it advanced with a love of order and of legality." [4]

To the Founders, liberty was not a new or abstract concept. It was a real, vital part of their daily lives. They had lived in relative freedom, even under British rule, and thus they were the more keenly aware when Parliament began to strip that freedom away. To the Founding generation, freedom was not a bargaining chip to be used to barter for privileges or material gain. Instead, they understood freedom to be both a right and a sacred responsibility, one to be

---

4   Alexis de Tocqueville, *Democracy in America*, trans. and ed. Harvey C. Mansfield and Delba Winthrop (Chicago: University of Chicago Press, 2000), 67.

guarded jealously.

They knew freedom couldn't preserve itself; it would survive and thrive only as long as each generation understood it, actively used it, and passed it on to the next generation. When the Founding Fathers were faced with the task of drafting the Declaration of Independence—and later, the U.S. Constitution and Bill of Rights—they drew heavily on their rich storehouse of heritage and history. Today, it is popular to teach that these documents were simply products of the age in which they were written, and that they are now mostly out of date. That is to be ignorant of many truths, including the fact that while times may change, human nature does not. These documents were not simply products of the 18th century, but in essence were the products of many ages and generations of thought and practice, and of trial and error. These documents accurately capture who the human person is and how we should govern ourselves, regardless of the age.

The Founding Fathers were keenly aware of this: They recognized that they had come to a critical moment in human history—a moment that would determine the character of ages to come. "You and I, my dear friend, have been sent into life at a time when the greatest lawgivers of antiquity would have wished to live," wrote John Adams to his friend and colleague, George Wythe, in 1776. "How few of the human race have ever enjoyed an opportunity of making an election of government, more than of air, soil, or climate, for themselves or their children! When, before the present epocha [sic], had three millions of people full power and a fair opportunity to form and establish the wisest and happiest government that human wisdom can contrive?"[5]

So where did the Founders get their principles? How did they know where to look as they drew up the blueprint of a republic? A detailed look at our heritage, as well as a study of the Founders' education, sources, and intellects, would take many more pages than we can use here. A brief summary of our heritage, however, would serve us well: we draw our moral, philosophical, legal, and cultural heritage primarily from what was produced in Jerusalem, Athens, Rome, and England.

What We Learned from Jerusalem

First, we owe much to the ancient Hebrews, a people whom God redeemed from slavery out of Egypt and brought into the Promised Land, Canaan, where He formed them into a sovereign and independent nation. Many of the earliest European settlers to America—notably the Puritans—borrowed much inspiration from the Old Testament record and imagery, as did later groups of great freedom fighters, such as African Americans and the abolitionists who fought to end slavery. From the Hebrews we inherited concepts foundational to our moral thought, like the Ten Commandments and the idea of moral awareness, that we as humans are accountable to our Creator. The most fundamental relationship in the history of time is the one between the Creator (God) and we the created. Out

---

5   John Adams, *Thoughts on Government* (Philadelphia: Pamphlet printed by John Dunlap, 1776; Boston: Reprinted by John Gill, in Queen-Street, 1776). Accessed online at http://www.pbs.org/wgbh/amex/adams/filmmore/ps_thoughts.html.

of all His creatures, God granted humans the gifts of communication and volition (the ability to choose one's own way), but He ultimately requires each person to account for his or her thoughts and deeds, whether good or evil.[6]

Humans, whether or not they choose to acknowledge this, are instinctively aware of an existence higher than their own, and of a law that rewards right actions and punishes wrong ones. The Founders drew from the Hebrews the idea of natural law, that there is an order inherent in the universe, that the Creator has instilled this order within the universe, designing it to operate according to certain laws reflecting His will. His patterns are evident in the changing of the seasons, the orbits of celestial bodies, the continual cycle of life and death, but also the benefits of obeying His moral laws as well as the consequences of disobeying those laws. He has given humans the ability to discern this order and these laws by observing these patterns in action.

Fundamental to the ancient Israelites' culture was the belief in the inherent dignity of every human being: As humans are created in the image of God, with reason, purpose, and will, the human is the only creature that God stamped with His own image. He has breathed His essence into men and women, making them superior to other living creatures. Though humans have corrupted their nature through sin, they retain, by unmerited grace, the identifying mark of God's image. Because of this, man has an inherent dignity that must not be violated. No man has a right to humiliate, defile,

---

6   Ecclesiastes 12:13-14

abuse, or enslave another, but instead has a duty to respect each person's rights, body and property. This is, of course, not to say that the Hebrews or the Founders were always faithful to this ideal; they, in fact, failed in various ways. It is because of these very failings, the inherent imperfections of human nature, that there exists a necessity for a higher law. In fact, because the higher law points out these failures, this can be a culture that had the ability to correct itself.

So then when humans rejected God's authority in the Garden of Eden, they fell from grace and became fallen creatures. This fallen and carnal nature, which is passed from generation to generation, provokes people to do what they *can*, not what they *should*. To preserve order in society, the Founders believed that man's fallen nature must be restrained through law, and that that law must be transcendent, an infinite standard before which all human beings, regardless of stature or wealth, must stand equal.

What We Learned from Athens

We have much to learn from the ancient Greeks as well. The Founders understood this. The works, sayings and deeds, especially of the great Greek philosophers and statesmen Socrates, Plato, Aristotle, Solon, and Pericles were widely studied, quoted and respected among educated American colonials. The ancient Greeks were one of the first peoples to intentionally organize their society according to democratic principles, though they were far from flawless: They treated women like property and owned slaves. Nevertheless, the Greeks recognized humans' rational capacity, a capacity that sets them apart from other living creatures. Humans alone have the ability, through reason, to discover qualities about themselves, their world, and the universe; they also have the ability to use this knowledge to improve their personal character and the communities in which they live.

The Greeks believed that the human is a social animal whose nature compels him to associate with other humans. They posited that, since no individual can achieve true self-sufficiency on his own, people must form communities in order to provide for themselves collectively and individually. The ideal of such a community, said the Greeks, is the *polis*, in which every citizen achieves moral perfection through his or her service to the collective body. This is, in part, a flawed notion. The *polis* does not produce moral perfection, but it is the ideal arena for an individual to learn to practice the moral law.

Importantly, ethics and politics were closely related in Greek thought. The philosophers believed that both the human soul and civil society operate according to the same natural principles. Both also require order. The Greeks believed that every society, and arguably its government, is essentially a reflection of the souls of its citizens. A citizen must tame the passions battling within his soul by cultivating a lifestyle of virtue; when citizens' souls are in order, civil society will follow suit. For a self-governing people to thrive and survive, it stands to reason that every citizen must first govern himself or herself.

One of the ancient Greek documents with which the Founders were well acquainted was Solon's Constitution, which "affirmed the reality of a 'polity'—that is, a system of government which respects the interests and the rights of all classes and elements in a commonwealth." Solon's Constitution was not long lasting, but it provided a valuable ideal that the Founders drew upon. Included in this constitution were the ideas of "checks and balances," compromise among interests and classes, and "mixed government."

Perhaps just as importantly, Solon's Constitution was based upon the idea that for justice to be achieved, the righteous man must keep his desires and responsibilities in balance, and so it is with the state: As a state is nothing but a compilation of many individuals, it must also keep its desires, roles, and responsibilities in check.

Solon's ideas of checks and balances and mixed government would make their way into the Constitution of the United States. The very basis of a true, healthy republic: a government of the people, by the people, and for the people, is the idea of individual self-government and self-control. While the Greeks would lay the foundations of political science and be the first people to discuss in depth the different arenas of human association, the Greeks would serve as an example of the merits of various political models but also of the tendency of man-made governments to succumb to tyranny. After a short-lived Golden Age of roughly 70 years, Greece failed, because the Greeks could not live together in peace and justice.[7] Though modern civilization owes much to the Greeks in regards to the arts and culture, America's Founders viewed the Greek commonwealth as more of a cautionary tale than a precedent worth following.

---

7   Kenneth Minogue, *Politics: A Very Short Introduction* (Oxford: Oxford University Press, 1995), 16.

What We Learned From Rome

Next are the Romans, a remarkable people of incredible military and engineering capacity. They would displace the Greeks, vaulting past them as Rome replaced Athens as the center of the western world. While the Romans tended to rule their non-citizens with an iron fist, they also pioneered the codification of law and made advances in the concepts of liberty, the separation of powers in government, and the balancing of the relationship between the individual and the state.

We inherited from Rome the foundations of our legal thought and the concept of the rule of law. Man's legal capacity, and the foundations of civil liberty, the Romans believed, were special gifts to their people from the gods, and was thus the inviolable possession of every Roman citizen. The Romans placed great emphasis on law as the safeguard of this freedom and the preservative of their unique culture. They believed, in the era of the Republic, that good laws protected the people from the overarching power of the state and also defended the state's authority against the whims of the people.

But perhaps more importantly, the Romans began to think of their nation as *patria* (Latin for "fatherland"), and this was a fundamental concept in their culture. This caused them to increasingly view the state as a benevolent parent who cared for the welfare of its citizens. They also began to believe that they had a divine mission to conquer the world; the state was the "being," so to speak, by which they could accomplish this mission and bring all peoples under the refining influence of what they would become, namely, *an empire.*

As such, the focus of Roman political life was the relationship between the state and the citizen. The state protected and provided for the citizen in exchange for his or her undying loyalty and service. Citizens were constantly reminded of their duty to the state by the public display of patriotic emblems, statuary, uniforms and architecture. But by shifting from a republic to an empire with the advent of the Caesars, the Romans set out on a path toward tyranny. Nevertheless, elements of the Roman Republic continued to influence Rome and its legacy for the western world. The notions of liberty and of the importance of the individual citizen were not completely obliterated. Even though these noble ideals were often only given lip service under increasingly authoritarian rulers, they remained touchstones and ideals, even if unrealized. For much of Rome's history, political power was divided among public officials and political bodies. Each class of citizens had power to elect representatives, and no single authority exclusively held power to make laws or pass judgment. As the republic became an empire, the forms were observed while the ideals underlying those forms became hollow.

But what can we learn, that the American Founders learned, from Rome's republican era and its fall? When Rome had a true republic, it was governed by a constitution that incorporated checks and balances and separation of powers. The important concepts of the separation of powers and the checks and balances in the Roman constitution were closely observed by the Founders and in many ways were imitated in the U.S. Constitution.

Our Founders were particularly attached to Marcus Tullius Cicero, the last and perhaps greatest hero of Republican Rome. Cicero was an eyewitness to the fall of the Republic and the rise of the Empire; he was an associate and acquaintance of Julius Caesar, Pompey, and Marc Antony; and he had a considerable influence on Octavian, who would later take the name Augustus. He was also a consul of Rome and was considered to be its finest orator. John Adams even had a nickname for Cicero: Tully. Cicero's influence, especially upon Alexander Hamilton and Madison, caused our Founders to create a Senate to check popular passions. It was also Cicero who taught the Founders that unchecked executive power must be avoided at all costs. To Cicero, natural law was this: Human laws are only copies of eternal laws. Therefore, human laws must be based on reason and should not conflict with the Divine, who is the author of reason and of the eternal laws.

In a universe where there is divine order and eternal laws, men are not bound to obey and follow unjust masters; by natural law, all men are born free and equal. Yet Rome fell from within because of the inward decay of its citizens. Centralization of power, class warfare, and the disappearance of a free-agrarian population (farmers working their own land and providing the foundation for a stable nation) all contributed to its fall. But all of those failings can be traced to the decay of the inner order. Rome's religion, based on gods all too human, and later emperor worship, could not provide the basis for lasting personal morality. With the fall of individual morality, the fall of the state followed in short order.

What We Learned From England

It was from the English that America largely drew its concepts of government, with one of the greatest contributions being English common law. The Common law, a body of non-codified laws, customs and judicial decisions that the English have traditionally regarded as their sovereign legal authority, was not the creation of a single individual or generation, but neither was it unmoored from the higher law of God. After all, England has a Judeo-Christian tradition, in no small way thanks to the significant role played by Catholic priests risking their lives to spread the faith early in English history but also to the influence of King Alfred the Great of Wessex (A.D. 849-899), who turned a primarily illiterate population into a more literate one, insisting on the people learning in the vernacular, using the Ten Commandments and the Bible as the primary teaching tools. This Judeo-Christian tradition heavily influenced legislation and judicial decisions that were understood to be based on that higher law. We must understand this lest we fall into the trap of the Progressives, who believe that laws are subject to the changing whims of human beings apart from the transcendent laws of the Creator. Because the common law is rooted in this natural law, it commands equal authority over all citizens: king and commoner alike. This rule of law protects the liberty of the individual, enabling him or her to exercise responsibly the rights to life and property.

As the Greeks had argued for the idea of self-governance, so too the English. But the English had an advantage the Greeks did not: the revealed truth of God's Word and the moral law it contained. The Christian concept that the English embraced was that every human person has the right and the duty to regard God alone as the moral lawgiver and the One who empowers human beings to live a good and moral life. Therefore, no temporal power has the power or the ability to exercise authority over a person's conscience, nor the right to violate his or her God-given liberties. Every person has a responsibility to consider his or her behavior and to conform to the moral law. This does not invite anarchy or unchecked autonomy. Rather, it bases law and self governance in the individual acting morally. Temporal or governmental authorities exist not to interpret the law according to their own whims, but instead to uphold the law by rewarding those who keep it and punishing those who violate it.

The English also further safeguarded the concept of self-governance by adhering to the maxim, *Quod omnes tangit ab omnibus approbetur*: "What concerns all, ought to be approved by all." They created a Parliament to represent the interests of the people before the King. At first, only nobles and the church could check the King's power, but eventually, wealthier merchants and professionals gained representation in government. They formed the House of Commons and, over time, universal suffrage emerged as Parliament formed into two chambers. Today, the House of Commons is the more powerful of the two, exercising both the power of the purse and the ability to make laws. The concept of an elected legislature with a higher and lower chamber like Parliament heavily influenced the design of America's bicameral legislature.

Over the centuries, as the nobles, the clergy, and the common people in England vied for power, each group filled a unique role within society, and the tension between the three barred any one of them from wielding too much authority. The power that they exercised collectively prevented the centralization of power within the government. This tension of power evolved into the concept of "checks and balances."

Out of Many Traditions, One

Popular rhetoric today attempts to convince us that the Founders were not exceptional men. They were motivated, we are told, by their economic interests, by their social standing, by their own self-interest, and that it was these interests that influenced the formation of our republic. While the rhetoric sometimes exaggerates these things, it is important to recognize that some of it is at least partly true—the signers of the Declaration of Independence, for instance, were indeed all white men. Some were farmers and tradesmen, but others, like John Hancock, were wealthy men. Some, inexcusably, owned slaves. They were imperfect men who had vices that are not to be glossed over or excused; it is important in our treatment of the Founders that we not turn a blind eye to their humanness. However, the remarkable feature of the Founders is that they were aware of this weakness—if not of their personal weakness, at least of the weakness of the whole human race.

This awareness, in fact, formed the basis of many of their most important decisions as they designed the American government. They also learned the lesson of human fallibility the hard way. We should remember that the world in which the Founders lived was very different from our own: a world much less diverse in the way that we understand "diverse" today. But our world today is so diverse precisely because of the ideas that these white, wig-wearing, imperfect men put down on paper.

The Founding Fathers did not have the precedents that we have today. No group of people had ever done what they did, which makes their deeds all the more extraordinary. It is precisely because they thought "outside the box" of their own generation that they were able to do what no one else had ever done. In 1776, when they wrote the Declaration, or even in 1787, when they wrote the Constitution, the Founders had no guarantee that their efforts would succeed, or that they would even survive. They could not put confidence in their manpower or their resources, but they could and did put confidence in their *principles*, because they knew they were true. How did they know this? Because they knew these principles were *transcendent*. The reason these principles have survived, prospered and stood the test of time is because they are *timeless* and *universal*. Our nation has survived and prospered because the Founders had the foresight and breadth of vision to look beyond their own communities, culture, generation and time and base our government on these principles. They looked back and learned from history what had worked and what hadn't worked. They understood the unflattering aspects of human nature, and instead of glossing over them, they confronted them and built safeguards against them. They were not naive nor utopian. But they built a new nation on principles that even they imperfectly understood and at times imperfectly applied.

Nevertheless, they knew these principles were true and that they were worth fighting and dying for. The time has come to renew these principles in our nation; we should come to know again these principles and learn to apply them in the age in which we now live. The United States of America has engendered more freedom and created more opportunities for more people than any other single nation the world has ever known. While our nation has continued to learn painful lessons from our experiences with injustice and prejudice, America has shown remarkable resilience, a capacity to learn from its mistakes, and an ability to continue surging forward more than any other people in any other time.

While every generation is shaped to an extent by its social and historical context, it is shortsighted to interpret the Founders and their principles this way. In fact, to do so would be grossly hypocritical, for we as a people have continued to operate on these principles—to great success both socially and economically—over the decades since the Constitution was signed. These principles took a small agrarian nation from the edge of the Eurocentric world and made it the greatest nation the world has ever seen. So the Founding principles must be worth examining, preserving and following, because we can tell a lot about an idea from the fruit it produces.

Our need today is not so much to return to the principles of the Founding as it is to renew them, to apply them afresh, in our age.

CHAPTER THREE

From Time Immemorial: The English Common Law

———————◆———————

In 1831, Frenchman Alexis de Tocqueville toured the young republic of America, studying her people and her laws in order to discern the source of her freedoms. One aspect of American freedom impressed itself deeply upon his mind: the relationship between freedom and the Christian faith. "[I]n America, it is religion that leads to enlightenment; it is the observance of divine laws that guides man to freedom," he concluded.[8] "Freedom sees in religion the companion of its struggles and its triumphs, the cradle of its infancy, the divine source of its rights. It considers religion as the safeguard of mores; and mores as the guarantee of laws and the pledge of its own duration."[9] By discerning the relationship between freedom and faith, de Tocqueville had stumbled upon a significant principle: In order to be free, man must be subservient to the law; and in order

---

8   de Tocqueville, 42.
9   *Ibid.*, 43, 44.

to be subservient to the law, man must acknowledge a law higher than himself—namely, an infinite and divine law, the law of God. According to the Bible, this law of God is evident to man through creation:

> For the wrath of God is revealed from heaven against all ungodliness and unrighteousness of men, who by their unrighteousness suppress the truth. For what can be known about God is plain to them, because God has shown it to them. For his invisible attributes, namely, his eternal power and divine nature, have been clearly perceived, ever since the creation of the world, in the things that have been made. So they are without excuse.[10]

America's Founders knew the Bible well; they were steeped, in it even if not all of them strove to live it out in their daily lives. However they would base their entire legal system on this principle: The moral law of God is inherently superior to any law of man. But how did Americans learn to apply this law to civil society—to everyday life? How were they able to enforce the "rule of law" without making it the exclusive property of civil authorities or church leaders? The answer lies in the English common law tradition that came to America with the first English settlers.

"[N]othing [is] more difficult than to ascertain the precise beginning and first spring of an ancient and long established custom," wrote Sir William Blackstone, the English jurist whose

---

10   Romans 1:18-20.

commentaries on English law were the most respected and comprehensive at the time of the Founders. "Whence it is that in our law the goodness of a custom depends upon its having been used time out of mind.... This it is that gives it its weight and authority; and of this nature are the maxims and customs which compose the common law. . . ."[11]

English common law, by nature, is difficult to define. An organic institution, it evolved over time from the ancient customs and mores of the English. Unlike civil or statutory law, the common law was unwritten; it existed from time immemorial in the hearts and minds of the English people and their judges.[12]

Before exploring the roots of the common law, it would be helpful to explain its constituent parts. First, the common law was *law* in that it consisted of a body of rules regarding social interaction. Like any sound law, the common law was meant to protect the rights and liberties of the people from hostile neighbors, external threats and government encroachment.[13] It regulated societal transactions, the judicial process and the use and ownership of property.

Second, the common law was *English*, in that it originated in England and developed according to the peculiar experience and "genius" of the English people.[14] For the English, the common law was a way of applying the transcendent principles of natural and

---

11   William Blackstone, Commentaries on the Laws of England, vol. 1, Of the Rights of Persons. Facsimile of the First Edition of 1765-1769, with an introduction by Stanley N. Katz (Chicago and London: University of Chicago Press, 1979), 67.
12   Robert D. Stacey, *Sir William Blackstone and the Common Law: Blackstone's Legacy to America* (Eugene, OR: ACW Press, 2003), 47.
13   *Ibid.*, 48.
14   Blackstone, 17.

revealed law to their particular circumstances and culture. This application most often took the form of case law.

Third, the common law was *common*, in that it was applied *to* all the people *by* all the people. The common law was not the property of a single person or generation, but rather, it belonged to the nation as a whole.[15] It recognized no class, rank, or title, but was applied equally to all men. Because the common law established a universal standard of behavior, it enabled people to govern themselves. If a king or ruler consistently abused his power, for example, the people had a right, according to the common law, to remove such a ruler and replace him with someone who would honor the law.

However, since the common law is both organic and unwritten, it essentially defies definition. Because of that, it would be helpful to trace the common law's origins. The common law springs from two sources: the Bible and natural law. Scripture, sometimes referred to as "revealed law," is the revelation of God's law to man. Since man is inherently sinful, God has given him the law of Scripture to live by, both for his own good and the good of others.

However, while Scripture is perfect and complete, God has also chosen to weave many of His truths into the fabric of creation. When God created the universe, He designed it to operate according to certain laws and processes. Collectively, these are called "natural law." Natural law not only reveals various aspects of God's character, but it also reflects the moral principles contained in revealed law. In

---

15   Stacey, 49.

his *Commentaries on the Laws of England*–which the Founders knew well–Blackstone describes this correspondence between the law of nature and the law of Scripture: "But as [God] is ... a being of infinite wisdom, He has laid down only such laws as were founded in those relations of justice, that existed in the nature of things antecedent to any positive precept. These are the eternal, immutable laws of good and evil, to which the creator himself in all his dispensations conforms. . . . "[16]

Together, natural law and Scripture form the basis for all just human laws. In fact, any man-made law that contradicts either of these is no law at all, but rather a corruption of the law.[17] "[The] law of nature," writes Blackstone, "being coeval with mankind and dictated by God himself, is of course superior in obligation to any other.... [N]o human laws are of any validity, if contrary to this; and such of them as are valid derive all their force, and all their authority, mediately or immediately, from this original."[18]

The unique origins of the common law set it apart from other kinds of human law. The codes that usually govern human society, such as civil or statutory law, originate in the minds of statesmen or legislators. But the common law originated *outside* of man and sprang up beyond the boundaries of any particular civilization. It is this almost other-worldly quality that lends the common law such

---

16   Blackstone, 40. The word "wisdom" is emphasized in the original.
17   Stacey, 51. Stacey quotes Thomas Aquinas, who discussed the authority of natural law in *Summa Theologica*: "Aquinas writes, 'every human law that is adopted has the quality of law to the extent that it is derived from natural law. But if it disagrees in some respect from the natural law, it is no longer a law but a corruption of law.'"
18   Blackstone, 41.

authority, making it superior to any monarch or ruler.

The common law gathered strength over time as people applied and adapted it to their particular circumstances. This gradual development afforded the people the opportunity to participate in the shaping of the law. We may safely presume that each application of the common law survived as precedent only because the people consented to it. John Davies, a legal theorist of the 17th century, described this phenomenon of "custom as consent": "[W]hen a reasonable act once done is found to be good and beneficial to the people, and agreeable to their nature and disposition, then they do use it and practice it again and again, and so by often iteration and multiplication of the act it becometh a custom ... [and] customary law is the most perfect and most excellent [way] ... to make and preserve a commonwealth." Thus, the common law is not so much good because it is old, but old because it is good.[19]

The common law was repeatedly tested and proven throughout its history. One such challenge and subsequent victory occurred in medieval England during the oppressive reign of King John (1199-1216). In 1215, on the meadows of Runnymede, a group of barons and bishops drafted a declaration of common law liberties and forced John to sign it. This document, called the *Magna Carta*, survived as a testament to the rule of law over the rule of man. Henry de Bracton, a legal scholar who served during the reign of John's son, affirmed this concept by explaining that all rulers actually derive their power *from* the common law. "The king himself," he declared,

---

19   John Davies quoted in M. Stanton Evans, *The Theme is Freedom: Religion, Politics, and the American Tradition* (Washington, DC: Regnery, 1994), 88-89.

"ought not to be under man but under God, and under the Law, because the Law makes the king. Therefore, let the king render back to the Law what the Law gives him, namely, dominion and power; for there is no king where will, and not Law, wields dominion."[20]

Centuries later, when the English Puritans embarked for the New World, they took the ancient common law tradition with them. Once planted in America, the common law flourished as the central institution of colonial government. Though neither England nor her colonies knew this at the time, the common law was destined to become the deciding factor in the approaching struggle between them.

---

20   Henry de Bracton quoted in Russell Kirk, *The Roots of American Order*, 3rd ed. (Washington, DC: Regnery Gateway Editions, 1991), 190.

CHAPTER FOUR

*A Self-Governing People: The Birth
of American Society*

———————◆———————

"[E]verywhere on the continent of Europe at the beginning
of the 17th century, absolute royalty was triumphing over the
debris of the oligarchic and feudal freedom of the Middle Ages,"
wrote Alexis de Tocqueville. "In the heart of that brilliant and
literary Europe the idea of rights had perhaps never been more
completely misunderstood; ... never had notions of true freedom
less preoccupied minds; and it was then that these same principles ...
were being proclaimed in the wilderness of the New World and were
becoming the future creed of a great people."[21]

As de Tocqueville examined the foundations of American
society, he was continually amazed by the "singular" people who
first settled its shores: the English Puritans. De Tocqueville saw
in the Puritans none of the characteristics typical of immigrants.
"Almost all colonies," he wrote, "have had for their first inhabitants

---

21   de Tocqueville, 42.

men without education and without resources, whom misery and misconduct drove out of the country that gave birth to them, or greedy speculators and industrial entrepreneurs." But the Puritans, he said, were neither adventurers nor malcontents. Educated and middle-class, they had no great need to improve their wealth. Upright and loyal, they cherished a great love for England and her laws. Even so, "they tore themselves away from the sweetness of their native country to obey a purely intellectual need; in exposing themselves to the inevitable miseries of exile, they wanted to make *an idea* triumph."[22]

This specific "idea" at the heart of the Puritan movement evolved over time. It began to take shape in the 16th century, when Henry VIII (r. 1509-1547) made England a Protestant nation by declaring himself Supreme Head of the Church of England so he could annul his marriage to his first wife, Catherine of Aragon. At the time, legislation was passed requiring all Englishmen to join the state-established Anglican Church. Dissenters, accused of disloyalty to king and country, were harshly persecuted.

Over the next several decades, various groups sprang up challenging the doctrines of the Anglican Church and protesting the inevitable corruption springing from the church-state partnership. One of the larger of these groups, known as the Congregationalists, believed that church and community should be patterned after the model of a covenant. According to Biblical definition, a covenant is a voluntary agreement between individuals and is made in the

---

22   *Ibid.*, 32 (emphasis original).

presence of God. Applying the covenant to their own circumstances, Congregationalists believed that every member of the church was equal, for all had equal access to the grace of God. After all, they said, the believer does not come to faith through bishops or priests, but through the Word of God and the work of the Holy Spirit upon a willing heart. They also argued that individual congregations should be allowed to govern themselves and to choose their own leaders. They supported their claims by pointing first to the example of the ancient Israelites, who lived under the Mosaic covenant, and then to that of the early church, which "had all things in common" under the lordship of Christ.[23]

As Congregationalist teaching spread throughout England at the beginning of the 17th century, both the established church and government leaders began to feel threatened. Church leaders were apprehensive of covenantal doctrine, for it not only encouraged individuals to seek truth from Scripture instead of from the clergy, but it also encouraged congregations to assert their independence from the state. At the same time, King James I (r. 1603-1625) feared religious dissenters for political reasons. Congregationalists were strong supporters of Parliament, for though they respected the king's authority, they believed that law was sovereign over man. They also adhered to common law theory, which taught that if any temporal authority violated the rights of his subjects, it was the people's prerogative to reject that authority.

The king and the church made every attempt to repress

---

23   M. Stanton Evans, *The Theme is Freedom: Religion, Politics, and the American Tradition* (Washington, DC: Regnery, 1994), 188. See also Acts 2:44-45.

covenantal doctrine and its adherents. Clergymen who preached
Congregationalist principles were deprived of their benefices.
Citizens who refused to attend Anglican services or who spoke
out against the state church were hauled into court and often
imprisoned. Congregationalists responded in one of two ways: Those
who chose to abandon the Anglican Church altogether were called
Separatists; those who stayed within the church, hoping to *purify* it
by their influence, were called *Puritans*.

The first group to contemplate emigrating to America
was a small Separatist congregation in the village of Scrooby,
Nottinghamshire. At first, the people reacted to persecution by
fleeing to Holland, which was known to allow freedom of religion.
While Holland afforded the people the opportunity to worship
freely, the Separatists had trouble relocating their trades to a foreign
market. They also feared the effect of Dutch "licentiousness" upon
their children.[24] As the years passed, they felt an increasing desire to
establish a self-sustaining community where they had room to grow.
But where could they go? Returning to England was not an option;
England had rejected them and their beliefs, and though they still
loved her as their native land, they now considered themselves first
and foremost to be citizens of Heaven. They believed that, just as
God had called the Israelites out of Egypt, so He was calling them
out of a spiritual Egypt and preparing them to enter a Promised
Land. But where was that special place? After much prayer and
consultation, the Separatists agreed that God was sending them to

---

24   William Bradford, *Of Plymouth Plantation: Bradford's History of the Plymouth
Settlement*, 1608-1650 (Enhanced Media Publishing, 2018), 24.

the New World.

The story of the Pilgrims, as this group came to be called, is well known in American history and folklore. However, an oft-neglected aspect of Pilgrim history is the uniqueness of the community they established in America. The Pilgrims were intent upon advancing the Kingdom of God in the New World and were determined to build their new lives according to the Scriptures. Therefore, as soon as they had sighted Cape Cod from the deck of the *Mayflower*, the Pilgrims drafted a covenant with each other, entitled the *Mayflower Compact*: "Having undertaken for the Glory of God," the document read, "and [for] the Advancement of the Christian Faith, and the Honour of our King and Country, a Voyage to plant [a] colony in [America]; [we] Do by these Presents, solemnly and mutually, in the Presence of God and one another, covenant and combine ourselves together into a civil Body Politick, for our better Ordering and Preservation."[25] Signed by the head of each household, this agreement defined for each person in the company his proper relationship to God and to his neighbor. Every member of the group stepped ashore already aware of his basic responsibilities as a citizen of the new American community.

Within 10 years, the Pilgrims would be followed to America by the Puritans, whose vision of purifying the Church of England had never truly materialized in the face of the established church and the state's oppression. This Puritan emigration, which in the span of a decade would number more than 20,000 people, was spearheaded

---

25   *Mayflower Compact*, Nov. 11, 1620.

by the visionary John Winthrop. A wealthy, prominent member
of England's Puritan community, Winthrop helped obtain a royal
charter to establish the Massachusetts Bay Colony. In 1630, he and
several hundred of the brethren sailed for America.[26]

Winthrop and his congregation felt even more keenly than
their Separatist predecessors, the Pilgrims, the pain of breaking away
from church and country. The Separatist community identified
themselves on the basis of their distinctiveness from the Anglican
Church, but the Puritans had long hoped for revival *within* the
Church of England. When that cause appeared hopeless, they rallied
around the belief that God had appointed them to leave the state
church and continue the work of His Kingdom elsewhere. Seeing
themselves as God's Chosen People, the Puritans hoped to establish
a model society that would serve as an example of holiness to the rest
of the world. This hope and belief is encapsulated in many ways by
Winthrop's sermon, "A Model of Christian Charity," that he gave
to his fellow Puritans aboard the *Arbella* while enroute to the New
World:

> We shall find that the God of Israel is among us, when
> ten of us shall be able to resist a thousand of our enemies,
> when he shall make us a praise and glory, that men shall
> say of succeeding plantations: the Lord make it like that of
> New England: for we must Consider that we shall be as a
> City upon a Hill, the eyes of all people are upon us; so that

---

26   Paul Johnson, *A History of the American People* (New York: HarperPerennial,
1997), 31.

if we shall deal falsely with our God in this work we have undertaken and so cause him to withdraw his present help from us, we shall be made a story and a byword through the world, we shall open the mouths of enemies to speak evil of the way of God and all professors for God's sake; we shall shame the faces of many of God's worthy servants, and cause their prayers to be turned into Curses upon us till we be consumed out of the good land whither we are going. . . Therefore let us choose life, that we, and our Seed, may live; by obeying his voice, and cleaving to him, for he is our life, and our prosperity.

Character of the Early American Township

Writing on America's early colonial period, de Tocqueville declared: "The general principles on which modern constitutions rest, the principles that most Europeans of the seventeenth century hardly understood ... were [by this time] all recognized and fixed by the laws of New England: intervention of the people in public affairs. . . responsibility of the agents of power, individual freedom and judgment by jury were established there without discussion and in fact."[27]

Upon their arrival in the New World, the Puritans began to build their communities according to the covenant model. The cornerstone of each village or township was the local church, in which every member of the community had equal standing. Each congregation elected its own leaders, and each was completely

---

27   de Tocqueville, 39.

independent from other churches in the region. Membership in the local church was required for those wishing to join the community; however, those who objected were at liberty to leave the village and establish their own community elsewhere. In England, this practice would have been impossible, as no unclaimed land was available. But in the vast wilderness of America, there was room enough for every individual conscience.[28]

The religious practices of the Puritans soon began to shape the character of their politics. Just as each church was self-governing, each village naturally asserted its independence from other villages. Just as every member of the congregation was expected to "work out his own salvation with fear and trembling," so every individual in the community was expected to behave responsibly as a citizen. [29] Just as each congregation elected its leaders, so every village began to elect its public officials, even to those posts which, in England, were still filled by royal appointment.[30]

These developments in self-government were an organic outgrowth of the way the Puritans and Pilgrims thought and lived their everyday lives and grew from a soil rich in Protestant doctrine and the English common law tradition.[31] Protestantism emphasized personal morality and responsibility, teaching that each person is directly accountable in his spirit to God. Similarly, the English common law established an objective standard of social conduct for

---

28   Johnson, 46.
29   See Philippians 2:12b-13 (King James Version).
30   Johnson, 71.
31   Russell Kirk, *The Roots of American Order* (Washington, DC: Regnery Gateway, 1991), 331.

all, thus providing a safeguard against tyranny.

These qualities produced a distinctly American strain of individualism. Because Anglo-Americans refused to acknowledge class or social status, no man was inherently beholden to another. Individuals could do as they pleased and were therefore free to voluntarily associate with others who thought as they did; the wilderness lay wide open before them. Uninhibited, such independence might have endangered America's embryonic freedom. After all, an individual who disdains all social ties will most likely take little interest in the community. Caring only for his own condition, such a man makes himself ripe for slavery. If a tyrant, for example, can convince the individual that he will provide for his needs, he can easily exert control over the deluded man's mind and actions.

However, the covenant model established by early Americans was designed to preclude this danger. The self-governing quality of the American covenantal community encouraged every participant to aid in its administration. The daily operation of the township depended directly upon the people; thus, it was in each citizen's self-interest to contribute to that operation. The township harnessed the energies of the individual in such a way as to involve him in public affairs and still keep him responsible for his own. This tension between the individual and the community protected the liberty of the people and allowed it to grow. This is one of the most important elements of the unique and emerging American idea of government.

The Colonies Founded and the Great Awakening

The Puritan groups of the early 17th century were at the forefront of a dramatic emigration movement from the Old World to the New. Christian peoples from all over Europe fled religious persecution to settle in America. Several of these groups, primarily those from England, obtained permission from Parliament to charter colonies, each of which developed distinct characteristics. Virginia was, of course, settled with the founding of Jamestown in 1609. The colony of Maryland was founded in 1632 as a settlement for Catholics. It would issue the Maryland Toleration Act in 1649, which was one of the first laws that explicitly defined tolerance for all sects of Christianity, and it is considered a precursor to our First Amendment. After the great Puritan revolt and the Battle of the Severn near Annapolis, the Calvert family managed to regain control of the colony in 1658 and re-enacted the Toleration Act, which allowed all sects of Christianity freedom in the colony of Maryland.

In 1638, Peter Minuit, the same man who bought the island of Manhattan from the Indians for trinkets worth $24, in conjunction with the Swedish government, would land with a band of Swedes near what is today Wilmington, Delaware, promptly calling the colony New Sweden. It was the Swedes who brought the quintessential log cabin design to America. Over the next nearly 60 years, control of the territory would shift from the Swedes, to the Dutch, and finally, to the English, then be annexed to Pennsylvania before becoming its own self-governing colony named Delaware in 1704.

In 1641, dissenting minister Roger Williams (1603-1684)

left the Massachusetts Bay Colony over disagreements with the governing authorities and founded Rhode Island and Providence Plantations as a refuge for religious outcasts. Pennsylvania (meaning literally "Penn's Woods"), a haven for Quakers, was established by royal grant to William Penn in 1681. In certain areas, several communities chose to join together for their mutual protection and prosperity. One of the first unions to be formed from such a partnership was the Commonwealth or "Public State" of Connecticut, established in 1639. In making a covenant with each other, the people of Connecticut set in writing the laws and regulations that were to govern the new state. This document, the *Fundamental Orders of Connecticut*, was the world's first written constitution.

The Carolinas would be settled in the early 1650s as settlers from Virginia moved south to create a buffer against the northward aggression of the Spanish. Eventually the port city of Charles Town, later Charleston, would be settled by several hundred English settlers from Barbados. The Carolinas would be split into North and South in 1712, with South Carolina eventually becoming a royal colony in 1729 with North Carolina following suit in 1744.

The colony of New Jersey would be founded in 1664 as a land grant from the Duke of York, later King James II, to Sir Carteret and Lord Berkeley for their loyalty to the Crown during the English Civil War. In hopes of attracting new settlers, they would put in place the Concessions and Agreement, a document promising religious freedom. New York would follow in short order in 1665, having recently been wrested from Peter Stuyvesant and the Dutch. By 1733, the last of the original colonies, Georgia, would be founded by James Oglethorpe. Oglethorpe's original vision for Georgia had been a colony for the relief of the poor, unemployed and persecuted Protestants. While in England, Oglethorpe was responsible for prison reform and the release of thousands of imprisoned debtors, but the idea that Oglethorpe founded Georgia as a debtors' colony is unfounded. He was far more concerned with the protection of the colonies north of Georgia, so the driving motivation for the settlement of Georgia was to have a "buffer state" or "garrison province" that would defend the southern part of the British colonies from Spanish Florida. Oglethorpe imagined a province populated by "sturdy farmers" who could guard the border; because of this, the colony's original charter prohibited slavery.

By the end of the 17th century, America was well on its way to becoming the most prosperous colonial establishment in the world. But as the country increased in material wealth, many of its inhabitants began to worry about the nation's spiritual condition. True, abundance was a sign of God's blessing and a natural result of living according to the moral and natural law, but abundance could also lead to corruption. Had not the ancient Israelites, in the midst of prosperity, forgotten their need for God? Had they not repeatedly broken their covenant with Him? Might not America do the same? Indeed, as the townships of New England flourished into bustling cities, the Puritan church diminished in its centrality to the community. For many Americans, "religion" increasingly became an affair of form and habit, no longer affecting their hearts. However, during the second decade of the 18th century, even as the faith of those in the cities grew cold, the peoples of the frontier began to experience a religious renewal.

In 1719, a Dutch Reformed minister named Theodore Frelinghuysen (1691-1747) began preaching revival sermons to his congregation in New Jersey. An emigrant from Germany, Frelinghuysen had brought to America a teaching called *Pietism*, which encouraged believers to concentrate on the practice of holiness in daily life. Pietism appealed to the practical people of America because it emphasized personal responsibility over one's spirit, and deemphasized abstract doctrines and creeds.[32] Many Americans began to reconsider their level of faith and to cultivate a practical application of it.

A young Puritan minister, Jonathan Edwards (1703-1758), responded to this growing spiritual hunger by preaching rousing sermons on God's holiness and His grace toward sinners. Revival began to spread throughout the New England countryside and beyond to the frontier. People gathered in fields and clearings to hear traveling preachers and to hold prayer meetings. George Whitefield (1714-1770), an English minister, set out on a preaching tour of the colonies, speaking in the open country to crowds of up to 20,000 people.[33]

This Great Awakening (1720s-1740s), as the movement

---

32   Johnson, 110.
33   Samuel Eliot Morison, *The Oxford History of the American People* (New York: Oxford University Press, 1965), 151-152.

came to be called, was characterized by its inclusiveness. Its simple message of spiritual renewal did not claim a particular religious denomination, nor was it directed to people of a certain ethnicity. Both the message and the response were universal. Before thousands gathered in the open air, Whitefield highlighted these themes:

> Father Abraham, are there any Anglicans in heaven?"
> The answer came back, "No, there are no Anglicans in heaven." "Father Abraham, are there any Methodists in heaven?" "No, there are no Methodists in heaven." Are there any Presbyterians in heaven?" "No, there are no Presbyterians here either." "What about Baptists or Quakers?" "No, there are none of those here either." "Father Abraham," cried Whitefield, what kind of people are in heaven?" The answer came back, "There are only Christians in heaven; only those who are washed in the blood of the Lamb." Whitefield then cried out, "Oh, is that the case? Then God help me, God help us all, to forget having names and to become Christians in deed and in truth!

As the revival spread, Americans gradually, almost unconsciously, began to turn their attention inward, away from Europe and toward each other. Up until the 18th century, most still considered themselves to be European, first and foremost. But with the advent of the Great Awakening, these Old World emigrants were reminded of what they had in common with each other. They were all a "Chosen People," having come to America to find freedom of conscience, to move about at liberty, and to build new lives in a land "flowing with milk and honey." They had come in order to live as servants of God rather than as subjects of a king. These realizations inspired Americans to look beyond their cultural and denominational differences; they began to see each other as fellow countrymen, working alongside each other toward a common goal.

Years later, de Tocqueville would explain this natural connection that arose between religious faith and American patriotism. "The greatest advantage of religions is to inspire wholly contrary instincts," he wrote. "There is no religion," he continued, "that does not impose on each [man] some duties toward the human species or in common with it, and that does not thus draw him, from time to time, away from contemplation of himself."[34] Christianity, he discovered, taught Americans how to reconcile individual liberty with a concern for the community. "Religion," de Tocqueville concluded, "which, among Americans, never mixes directly in the government of society, should therefore be considered as the first of their political institutions; for if it does not give them the taste for freedom, it singularly facilitates their use of it."[35]

The French and Indian War

As Americans enjoyed a spiritual revival, they also turned their eyes to the West. The open and mysterious wilderness beckoned to every man who desired to be his own master and work his own land. The frontier began to produce a new type of man, distinctly

---

34   de Tocqueville, 419.
35   *Ibid.*, 280.

American in his tastes and character: he was rustic, but not barbaric; intensely practical, but also intelligent. He lived in isolation from his countrymen, yet maintained a keen interest in political affairs. "All is primitive and savage around him," de Tocqueville would later write of this man, "but he is. . . the result of eighteen centuries of work and experience.... [H]e knows the past, is curious about the future, argues about the present; he is a very civilized man who, for a time, submits to living in the middle of the woods, and who plunges into the wilderness of the New World with his Bible, a hatchet, and newspapers."[36]

England encouraged this westward expansion, because it would, of course, enlarge and strengthen the British Empire. However, England was not the only European power speculating in the New World. For decades, the French had maintained trading posts and settlements both to the north and west of New England, and at various locations on the Mississippi River all the way down to Louisiana.[37] In the past, when the British and French had quarreled over American territory, the British usually came out on top, but they still had difficulty keeping the French off their land. At times, the French even provoked Indian tribes to attack and pillage English villages or settlements in order to discourage their expansion.

In 1754, the tension between the two nations exploded, almost inadvertently, into war. The trouble began when a group of speculators in Virginia, with support from the state, formed the Ohio Company to help develop the West. Suspicious that

---

36   *Ibid.*, 290.
37   Johnson, 125.

Frenchmen might be dwelling in the Ohio Valley, the royal governor of Virginia, Robert Dinwiddie, sent a militia to investigate the area. At the head of the regiment was a young George Washington, just beginning his military career. The regiment did indeed find French in the Valley. However, during the subsequent race to see who could build the first fort in the area, the English encountered hostile French soldiers in a field, and Washington ordered his men to fire.[38]

This small skirmish on the edge of the American colonies had momentous, global implications. Though few men were killed in Washington's scuffle, interactions between the English and French grew increasingly violent. As both sides returned injury for injury, the conflict escalated into a world war, fought in British and French territories all over the globe. The Seven Years War, or the French and Indian War as it was called in the colonies, would be waged from the Philippines to the American western frontier until the Treaty of Paris in 1763 ended the war.

Colonists enlisted for the war out of loyalty to Britain, but they were also motivated by their distrust of the French. France was ruled, in their thinking, by a notoriously decadent monarchy; the French people were locked into a severe class system which was retained even in remote colonies as the people looked to the king and government as absolute authorities.[39] These traditions were directly opposed to British notions of self-government and the common law. In taking up arms against the French, the colonists believed they were not only defending the Western territories, but also their political

---

38   *Ibid.*, 123-124.
39   *Ibid.*125.

rights as Englishmen.

Gradually, the conflict became a very personal one for Americans. Colonists living on the frontier were suddenly exposed to the combined fury of the French and the Indians. The enemy raided colonists' homesteads, burning farms and often slaughtering the inhabitants. Parliament, directing the war from England, failed to comprehend the plight of these subjects.[40] Officers sent to America from Britain were unaccustomed to the harsh conditions of the frontier and were caught off guard by the comparatively wild tactics of the Indians. In 1755, General Braddock's expedition aimed at the French Fort Duquesne (Pronounced "du-CANE" and now, modern-day downtown Pittsburgh) suffered a terrible defeat at the hands of the French and Indians near the Monongahela River. Braddock was killed, but young Washington managed to keep the British forces in a semblance of an ordered retreat. In the face of that defeat, the British withdrew to their "winter quarters," even though it was early July. The retreat removed all protection from the wilderness settlers of Pennsylvania, Maryland, and Virginia.[41] Such experiences forced Americans to rely on each other and to work together. They fought not as members of the several colonies, but as *Americans*, defending a land they believed had been given to them by Providence.

In the end, when the British and Americans finally drove the French into Canada, the war had accomplished more than simply securing the West for the British Empire. What the Great Awakening

---

40   Daniel J. Boorstin, *Americans: The Colonial Experience* (New York: Vintage Books, 1958), 361.
41   Morison, 162-163.

had accomplished for America spiritually, the French and Indian War effected socially and politically. Americans, already accustomed to self-government and united in their faith, now trusted their own judgment in the management of their affairs.[42] They were content to serve England as long as she, too, trusted their judgment and protected their liberty. That, however, was not to be: England had no intention of allowing the colonies to manage their own affairs.

---

42   Boorstin, 361.

CHAPTER FIVE

A New and More Noble Course: Revolution and Independence

———————◆———————

"The revolution in the United States was produced by a mature and reflective taste for freedom," wrote Alexis de Tocqueville, "and not by a vague and indefinite instinct of independence. It was not supported by passions of disorder; but, on the contrary, it advanced with a love of order and of legality." [43]

Contrary to popular opinion, the leaders of the American Revolution were not "revolutionary" at all. It is true that the members of the Founding generation were compelled to make unprecedented decisions in their struggle against tyranny, but their reasons for doing so were anything but radical. They fought not to establish a new order, but to preserve an old one. They entered the revolutionary conflict unwillingly and only after they had exhausted every other resource.

By the middle of the 18th century, America had the most

---

43   de Tocqueville, 67.

autonomous society in the world. While the colonists acknowledged the King and Parliament as their ultimate political authorities, with the colonial royal governors as the King's representatives, they managed almost all of their own affairs through colonial legislatures. These elected assemblies were responsible for collecting taxes, raising militias, and maintaining courts of justice. On matters such as foreign relations and international trade, the legislatures worked with the royal governors and Parliament to formulate policy. Colonial charters and the English common law were the main rules of conduct between England and the colonies. Americans were proud of their English heritage and traditions and counted it a privilege to be British colonies.

But the British, far removed from their subjects in the New World, saw the colonies primarily as an imperial commodity. America was rich in natural resources and manpower, and Britain was determined to take full advantage of them. But the refined gentlemen serving in Parliament knew very little about the American people.[44] Few if any of them had ever been to the colonies, and they were unacquainted with American customs and the colonial way of life. It simply did not occur to the British that the colonists would desire anything other than the honor of belonging to the greatest empire on earth. This was England's fatal mistake and it would ultimately lead to revolution.

The relationship between Britain and its American colonies first began to deteriorate in the aftermath of the French and Indian

---

44   Catherine Drinker Bowen, *John Adams and the American Revolution* (Boston: Little, Brown and Company, 1950), 211.

War. Military victory had come at a great price for the British. The conflict had more than doubled England's national debt, and now that Britain was the undisputed "owner" of America, she faced the daunting task of managing an empire larger than any other since the Roman Age.[45] Desperate for funds, Parliament looked to its lucrative colonies. Since England had gone into significant debt defending America, Parliament felt that the colonists should help pay the expenses. After all, the colonists had always paid far less in taxes than native English, and at the present time they were shouldering only a fraction of the public debt.[46]

So in 1764, Parliament passed the Sugar Act, aimed at enforcing steep import customs on sugar, wine, fabrics and other products. This was not the first time Britain had imposed duties on the colonies, but all previous regulations had been instituted for the purpose of protecting England's commercial interests. The Sugar Act was the first duty established for the express purpose of raising money.[47] The colonists were taken aback by this measure. One of the fundamental rights enshrined in the English common law was the right to be taxed by *consent*. Accordingly, the colonial legislatures had always assumed the responsibility of collecting American taxes. The Sugar Act sidestepped this provision and therefore marked a

---

45   Paul Johnson, *A History of the American People* (New York: HarperPerennial, 1997), 127.

46   *Ibid.*, 132. Johnson comments that, according to the British Treasury at this time, "the public debt carried by each Englishman was £18, whereas a colonial carried only 18 shillings. An Englishman paid on average 25 shillings a year in taxes, a colonial only sixpence, one-fiftieth" (132).

47   Arthur M. Schlesinger, Jr., ed., *The Almanac of American History* (New York: G.P. Putnam's Sons, 1983), 99.

dramatic departure from traditional Anglo-American policy. Several colonial assemblies appealed to Parliament for redress, but their petitions went unread.

To be clear, smuggling, privateering, and a booming wartime economy combined to create massive economic prosperity for the American colonists during the French and Indian War, so much so that historian John C. Miller argues that the war "enriched" the colonies to the point that British officials felt justified in collecting increased revenue.[48] With this attitude in mind, Parliament passed the Act, which was a tax on North American imports of molasses, sugar, and other products containing sugar. It also gave Britain a monopoly on the American sugar trade by allowing only British colonies to buy or sell sugar or molasses to Britain or other British colonies. They argued that the Sugar Act was necessary to maintain and strengthen the trade monopoly that operated between Britain and its American colonies, and that this was the main focus of the bill.

However, Samuel Adams, a chief protestor of the Sugar Act, argued otherwise. Adams argued that the Sugar Act was not a trade regulation but "a tax, levied for revenue, and designed as an entering wedge for parliamentary taxation of the colonies." Adams argued further that this act was a breach of the colonies' rights, and that it amounted to taxation without representation.[49]

The Currency Act of 1764 would be yet another blow to the idea of the colonists' self-governance. The Currency Act, an attempt to protect British merchants and creditors from depreciated

---

48   John C. Miller, *Origins of the American Revolution*, 89-90.
49   Miller, 104.

currency, outlawed paper money, affecting commerce for virtually the entire colonial population. Whereas the Sugar Act in large part targeted and affected the merchants of New England, the Currency Act marked the first comprehensive assertion of British sovereignty over *all* of the colonies, beginning a decade-long era of British posturing and grandstanding.

The following year, Parliament passed the Stamp Act, requiring every colonial document to be stamped with a seal purchased from a royal stamp office. The colonists had several grievances against this bill. First, it enforced a direct, internal tax on the colonies—something Parliament had never before imposed on Americans. [50] Second, it authorized a royal court of admiralty to try all suspected evasions of the tax. Courts of admiralty—originally created by the English to prosecute illegal maritime activity—were not required to call juries, and therefore deprived defendants of a trial by jury. Years later, this would inspire the Sixth Amendment in our Bill of Rights. In addition, the only court of admiralty in the colonies was located, of all places, in Nova Scotia, Canada; thus, every colonist summoned before the court would lose his right to be tried in the vicinity of his alleged crime. Third, Parliament voted to send 20,000 British troops to the colonies to "supervise" implementation of the Stamp Act. Adding insult to injury, the colonists were ordered to quarter these troops in their homes at their own expense, again, an experience that would give rise to yet another amendment in our Bill of Rights: the Third Amendment, which

---

50   Samuel Eliot Morison, *The Oxford History of the American People* (New York: Oxford University Press, 1965), 185.

forbids quartering of troops in private homes without permission. These gestures indicated to the colonists that Parliament not only doubted their loyalty as subjects, but also recognized the offensive nature of the Stamp Act. Benjamin Franklin emphasized this point in a letter to the editor of a London newspaper. Americans could forgive the Stamp Act, wrote Franklin, if they felt Parliament had passed it in ignorance of their feelings. However, the decision to send troops implied that Parliament was well aware that the Act would be distasteful to the colonists.[51]

During the previous year, when Parliament had passed the Sugar Act, Massachusetts lawyer James Otis had proposed that all of the colonies meet to discuss a collective response to Britain. Now that the stamp tax had been passed, the colonies agreed to act upon Otis' suggestion. In October of 1765, representatives from 9 of the 13 colonies met in New York City in what came to be called the Stamp Act Congress. The gathering was not a rowdy group of protestors, such as the British usually imagined colonial meetings to be. Instead, it was a gathering of distinguished gentlemen—lawyers, planters, and merchants: men of property and reputation.[52] All had been affected by British taxes, and all shared an interest in presenting their case to England.

The Stamp Act Congress wrote a letter to King George III, whom they acknowledged as the guardian of their common law liberties. Presenting their petition "with the warmest sentiments of

---

51   Benjamin Franklin, "Causes of American Discontents before 1768," *Writings of Benjamin Franklin* (New York: Library of America, 1987), 609.
52   Bowen, 280.

affection and duty to his majesty's person and government," the
delegates confessed, "[we] esteem it our indispensable duty to make
the following declarations, of our humble opinions, respecting the
most essential rights and liberties of the colonists...."[53] In their
appeal, the delegates presented several "resolutions" or statements of
their rights, explaining to the King how Parliament had violated each
one through the Stamp Act. The colonists argued that, as the King's
lawful subjects, they were entitled to the full rights of Englishmen.
One of these "undoubted rights," they explained, was the right *not* to
be taxed without their personal consent or the consent of their
representatives. "[T]he people of these colonies are not, and from
their local circumstances, cannot be represented in the House of
Commons of Great Britain," they explained. "[T]he only
representatives of the people of these colonies, are persons chosen
therein by themselves; and... no taxes ever have been, or can be
constitutionally imposed on [us], but by [our] respective
legislatures." The delegates claimed that it was "unreasonable and
inconsistent with the principles and spirit of the British constitution,
for the people of Great Britain [i.e., Parliament] to grant to his
majesty the property of the colonists." Addressing the King as the
"best of sovereigns," Congress solicited his help, expressing their
ardent desire to preserve a relationship with Britain both "mutually
affectionate and advantageous."

King George responded favorably to the Resolutions of the
Stamp Act Congress, but not for the reasons the colonists had

---

53   *Resolutions of the Stamp Act Congress*, 19 October 1765.

hoped. By the time the king received the appeal, he had other motives for reconsidering the Stamp Act. First, Parliament had begun to realize that the tax was impossible to enforce, and therefore an unwise use of money and manpower. Second, the tax had started to backfire on English merchants and businessmen. Suffering severe financial setbacks from American boycotts, many of these men urged Parliament to revoke the Stamp Act. "[W]e don't pretend to understand your politics and American matters, but our trade is hurt," wrote one politician on behalf of his district. "Pray remedy it, and a plague [on] you if you won't."[54] Third, Parliament itself was divided on the issue. William Pitt, a former Prime Minister, rose from his sickbed to address the assembly on this matter. "I rejoice that America has resisted," he declared to the House of Commons. "Three millions of people, so dead to all feelings of liberty as voluntarily to submit to be slaves, would have been fit instruments to make slaves of the rest.... [T]he Stamp Act [ought to] be repealed absolutely, totally, and immediately. . . because it was founded on an erroneous principle."[55] Many members of Parliament agreed with Pitt and insisted that the colonies were being treated unfairly.

On March 18, 1766, King George grudgingly signed a repeal of the Stamp Act. However, he did nothing to stop Parliament from passing more taxes later that year. Within several months of the Stamp Act repeal, Parliament had laid duties on paper, lead, paint

---

54   Member of Parliament for Yorkshire, quoted in Bowen, 292.
55   William Pitt (the Elder), speech in reply to Grenville, House of Commons, 14 January 1766. Beloff, Max, ed. *The Debate on the American Revolution: 1761-1783,* 2nd ed. (London: Adam & Charles Black, 1960), 100, 105.

and tea. The colonists again protested, writing petitions, boycotting English imports, and holding town meetings. In 1773, a town meeting in Boston was reportedly attended by nearly 8,000 colonists, all crammed inside the Old South Church.[56]

But it was a transformational act in December of 1773 that truly infuriated King George and Parliament. Masquerading as Indians, a maverick group of colonists calling themselves the Sons of Liberty boarded three British merchant ships in Boston Harbor and dumped nearly 350 chests of tea into the harbor. Outraged by what he saw as colonial impudence, the King pressured Parliament to pass a series of punitive measures called the Coercive Acts. The first of these transferred the government of Massachusetts from the colonists to the British authorities. Henceforth, every public official from the chief justice down to the local sheriff was to be appointed by the royal governor. Colonists were forbidden to hold town meetings or assemblies without permission. Parliament also revised the Quartering Act, ordering the colonists not only to shelter British troops but to also provide them with beer and rum. Lastly, Parliament declared that the port of Boston was now closed and would remain so until the colonists paid for the tea they had destroyed.

In September of 1774, nearly 50 representatives from 12 of the colonies met in Philadelphia for what would become the First Continental Congress. Like their predecessors from the Stamp Act Congress, the delegates wrote a letter of complaint to the King. In

---

56   Schlesinger, 113.

contrast to the humble tone of the Stamp Act resolutions, the tone of this document was more formal and resolute. Rather than being a simple petition, the letter was a "declaration" as well as a set of resolves. Making a clear distinction between the peoples of England and America, the delegates complained that, "since the close of the last war, the *British parliament*, claiming a power, of right, to bind the *people of America* by statutes in all cases whatsoever, hath ... expressly imposed taxes on them . . . under various pretenses, but in fact for the purpose of raising revenue. . . ."[57] Congress proceeded to list the Coercive Acts, claiming that all of them were "impolitic, unjust, and cruel, as well as unconstitutional, and most dangerous and destructive of *American rights*." However, the representatives still did not blame the King for their grievances, but this time faulted his ministers: "And whereas, assemblies have been frequently dissolved, contrary to the rights of the people, when they attempted to deliberate on grievances; and their dutiful, humble, loyal, and reasonable petitions to the crown for redress, have been repeatedly treated with contempt, by his Majesty's ministers of state." In closing, the delegates explained that "for the present," they would "prepare an address to the people of Great Britain, and a memorial to the inhabitants of British America [as well as] a loyal address to his majesty, agreeable to resolutions already entered into."

When the declaration arrived in the House of Commons, William Pitt urged his colleagues to consider its respectful tone and the character of those who wrote it. "[F]or solidity of reasoning,

---

57   *Declaration and Resolves of the First Continental Congress*, 14 October 1774. Emphasis added.

force of sagacity, and wisdom of conclusion, under such a complication of difficult circumstances, no nation or body of men can stand in preference to the general Congress at Philadelphia," he said. "I trust it is obvious to your Lordships that all attempts to impose servitude upon such men, to establish despotism over such a mighty continental nation, must be vain, must be fatal."[58] Pitt's warning fell on deaf ears. King George and his supporters in Parliament would not be dissuaded.

Early in 1775, the King declared Massachusetts to be in a state of official rebellion against the Crown and ordered British troops stationed in America to suppress resistance by whatever means they saw fit. In April, General Thomas Gage, the military governor of Massachusetts, sent British regulars into the countryside to arrest the rebel leaders John Hancock and Samuel Adams and seize and destroy any military supplies. A firefight at Lexington broke out with "the shot heard round the world," eventually turning into a running battle from Concord to Boston between British troops and thousands of armed colonists. It marked, in many ways, the beginning of the American Revolution.

In May, a sober Continental Congress reconvened to discuss preparations for war. The members drew up a declaration, *A Declaration of Causes and Necessity of Taking up Arms*, which laid out the "causes and necessity of their taking up arms." Outside of Boston, Dr. Joseph Warren, the young dynamic doctor who was

---

58   William Pitt, Earl of Chatham to the House of Commons, *"On Removing the Troops from Boston,"* 20 January 1775. Despite Pitt's eloquence, his motion to remove British troops from Boston was defeated in the House, 68-18.

serving as the President of the Massachusetts Provincial Congress, declared that England would never let the colonies go and that the colonies must raise a standing army of 13,000 men. Awakened to reality, the colonists made no more shows of loyalty or devotion to the king, but spoke in exasperated defiance. "If it was possible for men, who exercise their reason to believe, that the divine Author of our existence intended a part of the human race to hold an absolute property in, and an unbounded power over others," they wrote, "the inhabitants of these colonies might at least require from the parliament of Great Britain some evidence, that this dreadful authority over them, has been granted to that body. "But," they protested, "a reverence for our great Creator, principles of humanity, and the dictates of common sense, must convince all those who reflect upon the subject, that government was instituted to promote the welfare of mankind, and ought to be administered for the attainment of that end."[59] Because the government of Great Britain had failed in this duty, explained the delegates, and had insisted on violating their rights repeatedly, they were forced to change their appeal "from reason to arms."

It should be obvious to anyone that the colonists' appeal to reason and *then* to arms was directly related to their inherent rights as stated in the English common law: such beliefs had been imported to the American shores by British subjects who believed deeply in their inherent natural rights as Englishmen. Because of their religious beliefs and understanding of natural law, their decision to resist the

---

59   *Declaration of Causes and Necessity of Taking Up Arms*, 6 July 1775.

King's tyranny was an expected and understood reaction.

The members of the Continental Congress sadly confessed their belief that the King had been led astray by his corrupt ministers of state. "Towards the conclusion of [the last] war, it pleased our sovereign to make a change in his counsels," they wrote. "From that fatal moment, the affairs of the British empire began to fall into confusion, and gradually sliding from the summit of glorious prosperity, to which they had been advanced by the virtues and abilities of one man, are at length distracted by the convulsions, that now shake it to its deepest foundations."[60]

Despite the firmness of their resolve, the members of Congress even at that time indicated their willingness to reconcile with Britain, essentially offering King George and the Parliament a way out. "[I]n defense of the freedom that is our birthright, and which we ever enjoyed till the late violation of it—for the protection of our property, against violence actually offered, we have taken up arms," they insisted. "We shall lay them down when hostilities shall cease on the part of the aggressors, and all danger of their being renewed shall be removed, and not before."[61]

Nevertheless, any hopes the colonists had of making peace with Britain were crushed in the months following the *Declaration of Causes and Necessity of Taking Up Arms*. In June of 1775, the Massachusetts Provincial Congress voted to fortify the hills above Boston, most notably Breeds and Bunker Hills. The British, led by General Howe, realized their predicament: To allow the colonists to

---

60   *Ibid.*
61   *Ibid.*

occupy the heights and eventually place artillery there would force the British out of Boston. In the first formal, staged battle of the Revolutionary War, Howe's regiments would eventually dislodge the Americans off the hills overlooking Boston. In the course of the fighting, the British would lose more than 1,000 men, killed and wounded. Dr. Joseph Warren, only 34 years old and considered one of the driving forces behind the revolution, died covering the American retreat.

King George declared all 13 colonies to be in a state of rebellion and closed them to trade. In addition to sending thousands of British troops to the colonies, the king also hired a number of German mercenaries to "chastise" his rebellious American subjects. At this point, the colonists finally realized that King George had completely turned his back on them and abdicated his duty to uphold their rights. They were left with no choice but to withdraw their allegiance from Great Britain.

In the summer of 1776, the members of the Continental Congress wrote the *Declaration of Independence*. In that document they were careful to explain the general principles upon which they based their separation: "When in the course of human events, it becomes necessary for one people to dissolve the political bands which have connected them with another," they wrote, "and to assume, among the powers of the earth, the separate and equal station to which the laws of nature and nature's God entitle them, a decent respect to the opinions of mankind requires that they should declare the causes which impel them to the separation." They proceeded to lay a philosophical foundation for the declaration, which they encapsulated in five "self-evident" truths: "That all men are created equal; that they are endowed by their Creator with certain unalienable rights; that among these are life, liberty, and the pursuit of happiness; that, to secure these rights, governments are instituted among men, deriving their just powers from the consent of the governed;" and, lastly, "that whenever any form of government becomes destructive of these ends, it is the right of the people to alter or to abolish it, and to institute new government, laying its foundation on such principles ... as shall seem most likely to effect their safety and happiness."[62] These phrases reflect and encapsulate more than 150 years of American religious and political thinking preceding the Declaration.

The delegates proceeded to place blame directly at the feet of George III as they enumerated the many ways in which he had personally violated not only their liberties but also his common law responsibilities. "The history of the present King of Great Britain is a history of repeated injuries and usurpations," they declared. "In every stage of these oppressions we have petitioned for redress in the most humble terms; our repeated petitions have been answered only by repeated injury." They spared no words in their indictment of the King: "A prince, whose character is thus marked by every act which may define a tyrant, is unfit to be the ruler of a free people." Congress also blamed the English people for ignoring the pleas of their American brethren: "We have appealed to their native justice and

---

62   *Declaration of Independence*, 4 July 1776.

magnanimity," they said of the British, "and we have conjured them, by the ties of our common kindred, to disavow these usurpations. . . They, too, have been deaf to the voice of justice and consanguinity. We must . . . hold them, as we hold the rest of mankind, enemies in war, in peace friends."

Congress formally adopted the *Declaration* on July 4. This time, the colonists would not wait for King George to respond to their letter. They were an independent nation now, and they had a war to fight. The future was uncertain, but Americans realized the significance of their decision. The same week that Congress voted for independence, John Adams wrote home to his wife, Abigail: "I am well aware of the Toil and Blood and Treasure, that it will cost Us to maintain this Declaration, and support and defend these States. –Yet through all the Gloom I can see the Rays of ravishing Light and Glory. I can see that the End is more than worth all the Means."[63]

---

63   John Adams to Abigail Adams, 3 July 1776, quoted in William Bennett, ed. *Our Sacred Honor: Words of Advice from the Founders in Stories, Letters, Poems, and Speeches* (New York: Simon and Schuster, 1997), 64.

CHAPTER SIX

From a Confederation to a Federal Republic

———————◆———————

In October 1781, a young courier on horseback brought word to the U.S. Congress that the British had surrendered at Yorktown. After hearing the thrilling news, however, each delegate had to then contribute a bit of pocket change to pay for the messenger's services. They would have paid him from the treasury except that, at the moment, the nation's coffers did not contain enough to cover the man's costs.[64] Such was the state of the newly independent colonies.

The omen boded ill for the emerging republic. After declaring independence in 1776, the American states had established the Articles of Confederation, a system of government approved by the Continental Congress in 1777 and finally ratified in 1781. This system survived the Revolution but began to crumble in the years that followed. By the mid-1780s, the Confederation was hopelessly

---

64   Catherine Drinker Bowen, *Miracle at Philadelphia: The Story of the Constitutional Convention,* May to September 1787 (Boston and Toronto: Little, Brown and Company, 1966), 5.

in debt. Congress was powerless to defend the nation from foreign harassment; state legislatures were powerless to put down local insurrections. Finally, realizing that the country was coming to a point of national crisis in 1787 because of a dysfunctional system of government, delegates from several states convened in Philadelphia, determined to resolve these troubling issues. They emerged several months later not with a revision, but with an entirely new plan: the United States Constitution.

Why did the Articles fail? After all, under their authority the fledgling states had defeated the most powerful military in the world. The confederate system had effectively united 13 different societies into one nation, without disregarding any one state's unique traditions and institutions. The Articles had not initiated drastic reforms or introduced revolutionary concepts but had instead reinforced the established principles of representation and self-government. Why, then, did the confederacy deteriorate so soon after these successes?

Up until the Revolution, the American colonies had been accustomed to operating separately from one another. Each state had its own charter, government structure, and political history. Each state had different industries and commercial priorities. Most colonists had rarely even thought of themselves as "Americans," but as simply "Pennsylvanians," "New Yorkers," or "Virginians." During the war, for example, General Washington had ordered a detachment of New Jersey troops to swear allegiance to the United States of America. The soldiers were appalled at the suggestion. Their allegiance was to New Jersey, not to some body called the "United States."[65]

These strong state ties heavily influenced the writing of the Articles. Congress knew that in order to obtain the states' consent for the new plan they would have to tip the scales of power in the states' favor. Thus Article II of the final draft read: "Each state retains its sovereignty, freedom, and independence, and every power, jurisdiction, and right, which is not by this Confederation expressly delegated to the United States, in Congress assembled."[66] Practically speaking, this gave the states executive power. The central administration, embodied in Congress, was limited to governing the country only through 13 state legislatures.

Even with these concessions, the Articles did not meet with immediate approval. Many states still worried that any kind of central government would eventually grow tyrannical. But by the time the Articles were submitted to the states for ratification in 1777, the former colonies were already two and a half years into war with Britain. The ranks of the Continental Army, camped at Valley Forge, were diminishing rapidly from disease, starvation, and desertion. General Washington sent letter after letter to Congress, begging for help. "By death and desertion we have lost a good many men since we came to this ground," he lamented, "and have encountered every species of hardship that cold, wet and hunger and want of clothes

---

65   Ibid., 6-7.
66   Articles of Confederation, art. 2.

were capable of producing."[67] As the army's conditions worsened, so did the prospect of American freedom. The states could not afford to argue with each other now. The debate over independence was no longer confined to the convention hall. The enemy was on American soil, threatening American homes and lives. Such dire circumstances forced the colonists to lay aside state interests for national ones. By March 1781, the 13th colony had ratified the Articles, making it the law of the land.

Following the final victory at Yorktown, however, the states' "firm league of friendship" began to unravel rapidly. Having achieved the common goal of independence, the states turned their attention back to local interests. Without the cooperation of the states, Congress was powerless to collect taxes, muster troops, or regulate commerce. States quarreled over tariffs they laid on one another and over territorial boundaries. There was a multiplicity of currencies, with most states building their own armies and navies. "Our whole system is in disorder," lamented Alexander Hamilton, working as Receiver of Continental Taxes.[68] "It is neither fit for war or peace .... Held together by the slenderest ties, we are ripening for a dissolution."[69] Americans gradually began to see that the urgency of war, rather than the Articles, had fashioned the temporary bond between the states. This bond survived only as long as the British

---

67   Washington to Brigadier-General John Cadwalader, 20 March 1778, in *The Writings of George Washington*, ed. Jared Sparks (Boston: Russell, Odiorne & Metcalf / Hilliard, Gray, 1834), 5:290.
68   Alexander Hamilton, *"The Continentalist No. III"* in N.Y. Packet, 9 August 1781, in Alexander Hamilton and the Founding of the Nation, ed. Richard B. Morris (New York: Dial Press, 1957), 83.
69   Alexander Hamilton to James Duane, 3 September 1780, *ibid.*, 92-93.

expeditionary force remained. When the last ship of British troops left American shores, the Articles' inherent flaws came to light.

One fundamental flaw within the confederate system was its failure to establish a clear executive. At the time the Articles were being ratified, most state institutions had already been in place for several decades. No state was willing to sacrifice its traditions for a national figurehead or ruling body. Because of the peoples' insistence on state sovereignty, Congress found itself relegated to a position of relative servitude. The central government had no power to enforce the obedience of the states. Its meager authority extended only to the state legislatures and had no direct bearing upon individual citizens. Every federal "demand" to the states for taxes, troops or cooperation became what Washington described as a "timid kind of recommendation from Congress to the States."[70]

A second flaw, originating in the first, was Congress's inability to levy taxes. The country was deeply in debt by the end of the Revolution, but the government had no practical means by which to generate revenue. Congress could only *request* states to contribute their share to the national treasury. The states that complied were often late in sending their dues; some refused to pay at all. Without money, the government was incapable of promoting commerce, establishing credit, or defending the country's vulnerable borders. Congress's attempt to raise funds by printing fiat money backed by nothing but the promise of a weak government only caused inflation. Congress even pleaded with the states to grant her

---

70   Bowen, 5.

greater powers of taxation, but the states could never achieve the unanimity required to amend the Articles accordingly.

A third fundamental flaw in the confederacy was the government's inability to confront external threats to the system. Despite its recent victory over England, America was still susceptible to foreign attack. The British not only retained Canada but also maintained military posts along the northeast frontier, and even speculated for land along the Mississippi River. French trappers occupied the Mississippi Valley, looking for opportunities to enlarge their territory. The Spanish were eager to expand their settlements northward from Florida. At various times they provoked Native American tribes to harry and intimidate American settlers, so much so that Georgia, at one point, was forced to invoke martial law.[71]

However, Congress possessed neither the funds nor the men to meet these challenges. Each state had been assigned a quota of troops to contribute to national defense, but state legislatures were unwilling to risk the lives of their citizens for a weak and unpopular government. Congress's impotence endangered America's reputation abroad. Europeans observed the United States with curiosity but also with skepticism. They delighted in watching the states quarrel with one another, sensing that it was only a matter of time before the union collapsed and the land was again ripe for conquest. Both Spain and France anticipated seizing pieces of the territory they'd formerly held. Britain entertained hopes of reestablishing authority on the continent. True, Americans had beaten the British once, but

---

71   *Ibid.*, 31.

how could they in their weak state expect to forever stave off global powers?

In addition to affecting foreign relations, the weakness of the Articles also had serious implications for domestic policy. Without a strong central government to check their power, state legislatures misused their authority. Faced with a post-war economic depression, state legislatures imposed high tariffs on imports from other states. Well-populated states such as New York and Massachusetts economically exploited smaller neighbors, such as Delaware, Connecticut, and New Jersey. Many states issued their own currencies, printing huge amounts of almost worthless paper money in an attempt to boost their sagging economies. The resulting inflation was so severe that in some areas creditors fled from those who *owed* them, not wanting to settle debts with worthless bills. Rhode Island legislators passed regulations deliberately designed to line their pockets, earning them the nickname "Rogue Island" and prompting their neighbors to wish the state would fall off into the sea.

The final crisis came when bands of farmers, deeply in debt, began marching on state legislatures and courthouses. The largest of these insurrections, Shays' Rebellion, occurred in Massachusetts in the fall of 1786. Impoverished farmer and Revolutionary War veteran Daniel Shays rallied a crowd of malcontents and proceeded to chase judges from the state Supreme Court. The Massachusetts legislature lacked the resources to respond to the outburst. It appealed to Congress for help, only to discover that Congress, too, had no resources. A few months later, when Shays and a host of roughly a 1,000 men tried to seize a local arsenal, the state was forced to rely upon a privately funded militia to disperse the mob. Shaken by the incident, Americans began to reconsider the distribution of authority. The states had always opposed granting Congress too much power, but now they were realizing that weakness at the center spelled weakness for them all. True, excessive centralization could lead to tyranny, but extreme decentralization could lead to chaos or petty tyrannies. In order to survive, America needed to strike a balance.

The idea for a national convention to resolve the country's difficulties came from James Madison, a young statesman serving in the Virginia Assembly. In the spring of 1785, he orchestrated a meeting between his own state and Maryland to settle a dispute over control of the Potomac River. Delegations from both states met at George Washington's estate, Mount Vernon, to discuss the issue at hand. The gathering, called the Mount Vernon Conference, was cordial and productive; the two parties not only reached a consensus over the Potomac, but also patched up trade disagreements between the two states. Encouraged by this success, Madison suggested a larger assembly of states to settle unresolved commercial conflicts. In September of 1786, a modest convention met in Annapolis, Maryland. Though attended by only a dozen delegates from five states, the Annapolis Convention made a significant move. The delegates passed a resolution to summon representatives from all 13 states the next year to address the Union's critical condition.

Congress authorized the proposal but limited the convention's business to revising the Articles of Confederation.

At first, the wary states were slow to respond. Orders from Congress did not carry much weight, and it seemed more worthwhile to keep politicians at home where they were needed instead of sending them on some vague mission to Philadelphia. When the Convention opened on May 14, 1787, representatives from only two states, Virginia and Pennsylvania, were present. The assembly had to wait almost two weeks before reaching a quorum of seven state delegations. It would be months before others arrived. The delegation from Georgia had to travel more than 800 miles. New Hampshire did not have enough money in the treasury to send its representatives until August. Rhode Island never did send anyone.[72] Finally on May 25th, New Jersey's three delegates arrived, representing the seventh state needed for a quorum.

The Federal Convention Begins

It was a rainy Friday as the delegates gathered at the State House, now known as Independence Hall. They met in the east room, a room 40 feet by 40 feet, with the delegates arrayed around the room behind tables draped in forest green tablecloths, with three or four delegates at each long table. One of the first acts of the Convention was, by a unanimous vote, to elect George Washington as the President of the Convention. Benjamin Franklin, as the oldest delegate of the host delegation of Pennsylvania, had hoped to be the

---

72   *Ibid.*, 12, 13, 17.

one to nominate Washington. But due to inclement weather and poor health, he was not there on the first day of the convention, and the honor fell to Robert Morris, the financier of the Revolution and Washington's personal host during his stay in Philadelphia.

Everyone expected and assumed Washington would be the President of the Convention, and he was duly installed at the front of the room, where he made a short speech (hard to understand due to his wooden dentures), accepting the honor, but confessing he wasn't sure he was up to the task. Washington's role and influence at the convention cannot be overstated. His stature, and the respect in which he was held, was the glue that kept the convention together during the difficult times.

William Jackson was elected secretary of the convention, but James Madison appointed himself as the real secretary. He later wrote: "I chose a seat in front of the presiding member [Washington], with the other members on the right and left hands. In this favorable position for hearing all that passed, I noted in legible terms and abbreviations legible to myself what was read from the chair or spoken by members." Madison didn't trust the 28-year-old Jackson to actually take meaningful notes, and Madison was correct: Jackson recorded only official votes.

What troubled Madison in his study of ancient and modern governments in the months leading up to the convention had been his inability, due to scanty or non-existent records, to discern what the founders of the earlier forms of government had debated, discussed, and intended. Madison was determined that those studying the Constitution in the future would know *exactly* what the Founders had debated and intended. Over the course of the next four months, he literally did not miss a session of the convention and kept a journal that would exceed 600 pages of printed text; his handwritten notes were hundreds of pages more than that. At the end of each day's debates, Madison would take his notes, go back to his room, and write out fully what had taken place, sometimes writing out what would be the equivalent of 10 typewritten pages per day. It is because of the diligence and perspicuity of James Madison that we know today what took place at the Convention.

After electing Washington and Jackson, the delegates read their credentials and instructions from their individual state legislatures. It was a dry recitation of facts until Delaware stood up and read its instructions: They were not to agree to any change of the "one state, one vote" structure under the Articles. This was the first "shot across the bow" of the convention as the small states insisted that they have some form of equal representation in the new form of government. It wasn't a chance happening that Delaware had been given those instructions. The leader of the Delaware delegation, George Read, had insisted that those rules be given by the Delaware state legislature before the delegation left for Philadelphia.

One of the next orders of business was the laying of basic ground rules for the Convention. A committee was formed and rules suggested. First, gentlemanly conduct was to be displayed by all delegates: no gossiping and no speaking while another spoke. The committee on rules also suggested that the proceedings be kept secret, with nothing being said to anyone: wives, children, friends, or newspapers; essentially anyone and everyone outside of the physical room. Guards were posted at the doors of the Convention, and no one was admitted without signed credentials.

Many representatives in attendance had come expecting to simply revise the Articles of Confederation. But others, notably Madison and Edmund Randolph of Virginia, along with Alexander Hamilton of New York, had different plans. For some time, these men had been writing, speaking, and debating with their peers on the need for an entirely new form of government. While they agreed with many of the principles enshrined in the Articles, they believed the confederate system was too weak to uphold them. A loose association of 13 sovereign republics would not long survive. A government that communicated only with state legislatures would not preserve the liberty of its citizens. The only solution to the crisis at hand was to form a central government that affected the people directly and was strong enough to act on their behalf while not being too strong, so as to supersede the rights of the various states and individuals.

Madison and his supporters came to what was known at the time as the Federal Convention, prepared with a very distinct plan. Four days after a quorum was reached at the convention, on the morning of May 29, Edmund Randolph, the 33-year-old governor of Virginia, laid out the Virginia Plan, a series of 15 resolutions that did away with the Articles and replaced them with a strong, national government. Randolph had been an aide-de-camp to Washington in 1775, then became attorney general of Virginia in 1776, serving in the Continental Congress on and off during the War while establishing a large legal practice on the side. In time, Randolph would essentially become Washington's personal lawyer. He attended the Annapolis convention and then came to Philadelphia as the newly elected governor of Virginia.

"Mr. Speaker," Randolph began that morning, "it is my regret that the task has fallen on me to introduce the great subject of our mission. I lament the crisis that revising the federal system has brought about, but I believe that it is necessary to prevent the fulfillment of the prophecies of an imminent American downfall that some of our compatriots have offered. Although I am quite sure that the authors of the Articles of Confederation had the best interests of the Union in mind, the concepts of constitutions and confederacies were still in their infant stages, and those patriot citizens had never experienced such crises as the commercial discord that has arisen among the states, a rebellion such as what was witnessed in Massachusetts, foreign debts becoming urgent, treaties being violated, and the havoc of paper money." [73]

Randolph went on to describe in detail the specific deficiencies with the Articles and then proposed the new plan designed by Madison, as well as himself, all with Washington's blessing. The Virginia Plan called for three branches: legislative,

---

73   James Madison's copious notes of the Federal Convention, known also as the Constitutional Convention, allow us to understand what was being debated for those nearly four months in Philadelphia. In an attempt to make the debates come alive, the debates in this book have been put into a more active voice. The quotes of the various delegates from the Convention are the words they spoke and one can access Madison's notes, broken out day-by-day, at the Yale Law School's the Avalon Project: https://avalon.law.yale.edu/subject_menus/debcont.asp

executive, and judicial. The legislature would be the most powerful branch: It would decide who would serve in the executive and judicial branches. In addition, the legislative branch would be *bicameral*, with the House of Representatives elected by the people and the Senate elected by the House. In the Virginia Plan, representation in the House and Senate would be based on population, and it was the issue of representation that would prove to be a sticking point with the small states. In addition, the Virginia Plan called for the legislature to regulate interstate trade, something the national Congress was not able to do under the Articles. The new government called for also would be allowed to strike down laws deemed unconstitutional, veto state legislation, and use armed forces to enforce laws.

When Randolph finished that day, it was said the room sat in complete silence. Most of the representatives had come expecting to hear creative proposals, but this plan had sweeping implications they had never thought of.[74] The small-state men, the defenders of the Articles, sat stunned by what they had heard. Many had just arrived in Philadelphia days before, having come to revise the Articles of Confederation. Instead, they were taken by surprise by the federalists. What they had just heard was not even a radical revision of the Articles; it was a complete *elimination* of the Articles, and in their place would be a strong, centralized government.

As soon as Randolph was done, Madison and other allies, taking advantage of the momentum, began debating the plan,

---

74   *Ibid.*, 38.

pushing immediately the idea of proportional representation. Madison was determined that two great injustices would be dealt with at the Convention: the issue of equal representation among the states, and the power of the state legislatures. The large states resented the smaller states exacting more power and control in the Confederation Congress than their size and population warranted: Virginia, Massachusetts, and Pennsylvania had 45% of the nation's population, but less than 25% of the power in the national government. It just didn't seem fair at face value, and the large states had had enough: They were determined to get rid of the equal vote for every state.

To Madison, the injustice of equal representation for every state was patently obvious: Why should a small state like Delaware, a tenth of the size of Virginia, have equal power in the national government? Were Delaware's citizens really ten times more valuable and powerful than Virginia's? Madison was determined to deal with the injustice of the equal representation and also to put the power of the new government more in the hands of the people, thereby undercutting even more the power of state legislatures in the national government.

Caught off guard by Randolph's motion, the small states were not ready with a response. Because of their lack of preparation and of the initiative taken by Randolph, the Virginia Plan was to set the agenda for the remainder of the Convention. Had the small-state, Anti-Federalist men come prepared with a plan at the outset of the convention, perhaps the results might have been different. But the big-state Federalists came with a plan and set the tone, and in many ways, the terms, of the convention and the resulting Constitution.

The following morning, before the small-state men could respond to the Virginia Plan, Randolph was back on his feet. It had been recommended to him, he said, by Gouverneur Morris of Pennsylvania, that he alter the wording of his first resolution. As it stood, the resolution proposed that the Articles be "corrected and enlarged" to more effectively fulfill their role. But Mr. Morris had made a more radical suggestion. Let it read, he said, "that a Union of the States merely federal will not accomplish the objects proposed by the articles of Confederation," and "that a national Government ought to be established consisting of a supreme Legislative, Executive & Judiciary."[75]

Once again, the delegates sat in baffled silence. Every delegate present understood the significance of the suggestion, but it had come to the floor so abruptly that no one knew how to respond. The outcome of the Convention hinged on this fundamental distinction between "federal" and "national." A federal system, such as the Articles embodied, was a loose compact between its members. It rested merely upon the "good faith" of the states, trusting them to defend each other willingly and to sacrifice their own interests for those of the whole. The Articles had demonstrated beyond a doubt the feebleness of such a system. Yet the alternative, a national government, made the small-state men shake in their boots. "National" meant a strong, impersonal, central government,

---

75   *Debates in the Federal Convention of 1787*, recorded by James Madison, May 30.

miles away, potentially unable and unwilling to sympathize with the particular needs of its subjects. How would the smaller states compete with their larger neighbors at the national level?

The small-state men challenged Mr. Morris' idea. What, exactly, did he mean by a "national" government? "[I]n all communities there must be one supreme power, and one only," responded Morris. While a federal system can act only through the states, he said, an effective national government has "a compleat and compulsive operation" over them. Such strong words made several members shift in their seats. Roger Sherman of Connecticut acknowledged that the Articles had, indeed, proven themselves deficient in many respects, but he did not consider these grounds for abandoning the system altogether. After all, establishing a "compleat and compulsive" central government would entail dramatic changes. In what manner, for example, would the people be represented under this new arrangement?

In answer to this query, the delegates consulted Mr. Randolph's plan. Resolve 2 addressed representation: "[T]he rights of suffrage in the National Legislature ought to be proportioned to the quotas of contribution, or to the number of free inhabitants." George Read of Delaware promptly declared: "Mr. Chairman, I move that the whole debate of representation be postponed. I remind the committee that the state of Delaware is restrained by their constitutional commission from agreeing to any change in representation and that should a change be agreed upon, it might become our duty to retire from the convention."[76] Alarmed at the prospect of losing its fragile quorum so early in the proceedings, the house voted to adjourn for the day to permit liberal discussion.

The free afternoon and evening gave the members a chance to clear their heads and come to grips with the issues at hand. Certainly, none were unaccustomed to political wrangling; every member at the Convention had brought with him years of experience. Over three-fourths of their number had served in the Continental Congress, and several had sat in state assemblies. Seven were former or current governors, and eight had signed the Declaration of Independence. Each was strong in his convictions but also skilled in the art of compromise. In addition, every man knew that beyond his opponents in the Convention were adversaries far more powerful and menacing. The nations of Europe took it as a matter of course that the American union would soon dissolve, leaving the states unprotected against foreign invasion. Indeed, word from abroad was not encouraging. John Adams, serving as ambassador in London, had recently sent word that British ministers refused to negotiate with the Confederacy, believing it nearer to collapse with each passing day.[77]

Perhaps these harsh realities weighed upon the delegates' minds as they reconvened the following day. Something must have impressed them, for even the small-state men seemed suddenly open to discussion of a national government. Almost immediately after Washington opened the session, the Convention passed a

---

76   *Ibid.*
77   Bowen, 26.

resolution establishing a bicameral legislature, consisting of a House of Representatives and a Senate. This measure required little debate; even though the Articles had appointed only one legislative body, nearly every state legislature contained two houses so it was a natural solution for the national government.

However, talk then turned to the mode of election for these assemblies. Under the Articles, members of Congress were appointed by the state legislatures. In contrast, the Virginia Plan prescribed popular election for the House, and election by the House for the Senate, thereby entirely eliminating state legislatures from the process. Roger Sherman would protest that this gave too much power to the uneducated public. "The people immediately should have as little to do as may be about the Government," he said. "They want [for] information and are constantly liable to be misled."

Elbridge Gerry, whose native Massachusetts had so recently suffered from "the people" in Shays' Rebellion, heartily agreed. "The evils we experience flow from the excess of democracy. The people do not want virtue, but are the dupes of pretended patriots."[78] George Mason of Virginia countered both of them, arguing that a branch drawn directly from the people would identify with their needs more readily than would an assembly chosen by their superiors. Madison agreed, saying that he "considered the election of one branch of the National Legislature as essential to every plan of free Government." He acknowledged Gerry's fears of popular ignorance, and supported a course of "successive filtrations" in the election of other officers,

---

78   Ralph Ketcham, ed., *The Anti-Federalist Papers and the Constitutional Convention Debates* (New York: Mentor, 1986), 39, 40.

but considered it vital to the strength of the republic that at least one legislative body be chosen by the people directly.[79] Mason and Madison's arguments must have satisfied enough of the small-state men, for the assembly proceeded to pass the resolution on popular election for the House.

Over the next two weeks, the convention moved from one topic to the next, arguing over everything from a national veto on state laws to government salaries. Although the sessions were long and the debates seemingly interminable, the several states were able to agree on a remarkable number of issues. By mid-June, the small-states had even won the fight to give state legislatures control over senatorial elections. However, once they achieved this victory, the small-states grew more demanding. Concerned that proportional representation would sap their power against the large states, they began to insist upon equal representation not only in the Senate but also in the House. Under a system of proportionate representation, declared David Brearly of New Jersey, the three most populous states—Virginia, Pennsylvania, and Massachusetts—would effectively dictate policy for the other ten. "Judging of the disparity of the States by the quota of Congress," he said, "Virginia would have 16 votes, and Georgia, but one."[80] Would this not be unjust, asked the small states? Would this not produce a tyranny of the greater states against the lesser?

The small states were defending familiar territory. Under the Articles of Confederation, each state had exercised a single vote. Armed with this precedent, the small-state men increasingly

---

79   *Ibid.*, 41.
80   Madison Debates, June 9.

emphasized the need to preserve the confederate model. William Paterson of New Jersey declared that if the delegates abandoned the Articles for a new plan, they would be violating the Convention's purpose. Many states had specifically commissioned their representatives *only* to revise the Articles. "We must not transgress these boundaries," warned Paterson, "or we should be charged by our Constituents with usurpation."[81]

The Small-State Men Strike Back

On Monday, June 11, Sherman was the first small-state man to truly respond and offer any direct alternatives to the Virginia Plan. In his early 60s, Sherman was one of the older delegates at the Convention. He had been called a variety of things: "that old Puritan," "honest as an angel," "wily as the devil," "slippery as an eel," "rigged as a buckram," Sherman was, nevertheless, well respected. He had begun life as a cobbler but trained himself in law and was a member of the State Supreme Court of Connecticut. And though he was one of the more frequent speakers at the Convention, he was laconic by nature. Once, when asked to speak at the dedication of a new bridge, he walked out on the bridge, looked around, patted the handrail, looked back at the crowd, and said, "This seems to be a good bridge," and then walked off the bridge— and that was the entirety of his dedication speech that day!

What Sherman wanted was equal footing for the smaller states in some part of the new government proposed. He wanted the

---

81   *Ibid.*

lower house to be based on population, but the upper house to give one vote to every state, regardless of population. Sherman, William Paterson and other small-state men wanted what the small states had with the Confederation Congress: equal voting for every state, regardless of population.

The big-state men, however, were not interested in the least in Sherman's plan. They assumed they had the upper hand at the Convention: the Virginia Plan had sailed through the Committee of the Whole, and although not officially passed by the actual Convention, it was all the Convention had been debating for two weeks. The big states thought they had the advantage, the truth, and the facts, and they were not about to accept a compromise.

In response to Sherman's proposal, not only did the big-state men not even respond to his ideas, but James Wilson of Pennsylvania, a Scottish immigrant who signed the Declaration of Independence and a future associate justice on the United States Supreme Court, replied, "Mr. Chairman, I move that the right of suffrage in the second branch ought to be according to the same rule as in the first branch." There would be no equal votes for the states in the new form of government if the big-state men could help it.

Rufus King of Massachusetts seconded the idea that the rules of representation ought not to be according to the rules established in the Articles, and a vote was taken in the Committee of the Whole on proportional representation in the lower house. It passed, seven states to three, with Maryland divided (and of course New Hampshire not yet in attendance). Sherman almost immediately moved that a vote be held on representation in the upper house, warning that "the small states would never agree to a plan on any other principle than an equality of suffrage in this branch."

The vote went to the Committee of the Whole, and the big states won that one too, six states to five, with James Madison the driving force behind the defeat of Sherman's proposal. On June 13, Madison called for a Convention vote on the Virginia Plan: He figured it had passed once already, and the two votes on representation had been carried by the big-state men. It would carry again. But Madison mis-read the situation entirely.

On June 14, William Paterson addressed the convention and told the gathered delegates that it was the wish of New Jersey and others to have more time to contemplate the plan reported on from the Committee of the Whole. What was really taking place was that Paterson was stalling. For weeks, the small-state men had been battered and pushed around by the big-state men, debating and arguing the big states' chosen plan, and often losing the debates. What Paterson wanted was a little time to pull together a rebuttal plan and give the small-state men their own plan, their own flag around which to fight. The delegates from New Jersey, Connecticut, Delaware, and New York (sans Hamilton), as well as Luther Martin of Maryland banded together, led by Paterson, to come up with their own plan. Suddenly the Convention hung in the balance. John Dickinson of Delaware informed Madison that "this was the consequence of pushing things too far." The small states, rallying behind Paterson, decided to request a day off from the Convention in order to prepare an alternative to the Virginia Plan.

When the assembly met again on June 15, Paterson presented to the Convention a nine-point revision of the Articles of Confederation. The proposal, called the New Jersey Plan, after Paterson's state, preserved the independence of the states from a central government. While the Virginia Plan appointed a bicameral legislature, a single executive, and proportional representation, the New Jersey Plan proposed a single legislative body, a plural executive, and equal representation. The Virginia Plan designed a government that operated directly upon the people; the New Jersey plan, a government that worked through the state legislatures.

Unfortunately for the small states, their advocates had waited far too long to build support at the Convention. By this time, most of the delegates were convinced that the Articles needed to be replaced by a stronger system. The Convention debated the New Jersey Plan for only two days before Madison dismantled and trounced it in a long speech, and the Convention voted it down. Nevertheless, the small states refused to surrender in their fight for equal representation. Likewise, the large states would not give up proportional representation. As the days passed, compromises were repeatedly rejected, and debate turned into diatribe.

Jonathan Dayton of New Jersey described the Virginia Plan as "a novelty, an amphibious monster that will never be received by the people."[82] John Dickinson, representing Pennsylvania at the convention, snapped that "If the General Government should be

---

82   Bowen, 130.

left dependent on the State Legislatures, it would be happy for us if we had never met in this room."[83] Small-state defender Gunning Bedford, a tall and heavy man from Delaware, worked himself into a frenzy: "You insist that you will never hurt or injure the lesser states. I do not, gentlemen, trust you! We have been told with a dictatorial air that this is the last moment for a fair trial in favor of good government. It will be the last, indeed, if the propositions reported from the Committee go forth to the people. The large states dare not dissolve the confederation, if they do the small ones will find a foreign ally of more honor and more good faith who will take them by the hand and do them justice. You will annihilate your federal government, and ruin must stare you in the face!"

The conflict grew so fierce that Benjamin Franklin, 81 years old at the time of the Convention, who had spoken little so far, rose and addressed the convention:

> The small progress we have made after 4 or 5 weeks close attendance and continual reasonings with each other; our different sentiments on almost every question, producing almost as many noes as ayes, is methinks a melancholy proof of the imperfection of the human understanding. We indeed seem to feel our own want of political wisdom, since we have been running about in search of it. We have gone back to ancient history for models of government, and examined the different forms of those republics which, having been formed with the seeds of their own

---

83   *Ibid.*, 185.

dissolution, now no longer exist. And we have viewed modern states all round Europe, but find none of their constitutions suitable to our circumstances.

In this situation of this assembly, groping as it were in the dark to find political truth, and scarce able to distinguish it when presented to us, how has it happened Sir, that we have not hitherto once thought of humbly applying to the Father of lights to illuminate our understanding? In the beginning of the contest with Great Britain, when we were sensible of danger, we had daily prayers in this room for Divine protection. Our prayers were heard and they were graciously answered. All of us engaged in this struggle must have observed frequent instances of the superintending providence in our favor. To that kind providence we owe this happy opportunity of consulting in peace on the means of establishing our future national felicity. And have we now forgotten this powerful friend? Or do we imagine we no longer need His assistance?

I have lived, sir, a long time, and the longer I have lived, the more convincing proofs I see of this truth, that God governs the affairs of men. If a sparrow cannot fall to the ground without His notice, is it probable that an empire can rise without his aid? We have been assured in the sacred writings that "except the Lord build the house, they labor in vain that build it. I firmly believe this, and I also believe without his concurring aid we shall succeed in this political building no better than the builders of Babel. We shall be divided by our little partial local interests; our projects will be confounded and we ourselves shall become a reproach and bye word down to future ages. And what is worse, mankind may hereafter from this unfortunate instance despair of establishing government by human wisdom and leave it to chance, war and conquest. I therefore beg leave to move that henceforth prayers imploring the assistance of Heaven, and its blessings on our deliberations, be held in this Assembly every morning before we proceed to business, and that one or more of the Clergy of this City be requested to officiate in that Service.

The discouraged delegates appreciated Franklin's suggestion for morning prayers but knew there was a distinct problem with the proposal: The convention had no money with which to pay a chaplain.[84]

In this disheartened state the delegates adjourned for two days to celebrate the Fourth of July. Outside, the streets of Philadelphia were filled with patriotic merrymakers. The delegates were feted and applauded by admiring constituents. "The Federal Convention—" toasted party after party, "—may the result of their meeting be as glorious as its members are illustrious!"[85] The delegates, sworn to secrecy on their proceedings, forced smiles and raised their glasses along with everyone else.

After the holiday, the delegates reconvened to more squabbling and a stronger deadlock. On July 10, George Washington wrote to Alexander Hamilton, who had returned to New York

---

84   *Ibid.*, 126, 127, 131.
85   *Ibid.*, 139.

several days previously, "You will find but little ground [here] on which the hope of a good establishment can be formed. I almost despair of seeing a favorable issue to the proceedings of the Convention, and do therefore repent of having had any agency in the business."[86] At this time, Luther Martin of Maryland wrote in his journal, "Now [the beginning of July] the convention is hanging by a thread." Nathaniel Gorham of Massachusetts even proposed that the large states have their state lines redrawn and reapportioned to balance the power between the states. Lansing and Yates from New York left the Convention altogether in protest.

---

86   *Ibid.*, 140.

CHAPTER SEVEN
"We the People of the United States"

————————◆————————

As the Convention entered the second week of July, it had become very clear that some form of equal representation in the proposed new government was the "line drawn in the sand" for the small states at the Constitutional Convention. As a matter of principle, the large states were refusing to give the small states equal representation, while the smaller states wouldn't budge until they had that. About this time, as it appeared the Convention might begin to truly fracture, Oliver Ellsworth of Connecticut brought back Sherman's proposal presented earlier in the Convention. Sherman had observed that England's House of Lords possessed a vote equal with the House of Commons for the purpose of protecting its rightful authority. Why should not this be the case in the American legislature? Let the House grant votes to each state according to population, but let the Senate allow each state one vote only.[87]

The first time Sherman had advanced this proposal, it

---

87   Madison Debates, July 7.

was not even taken up for a vote. But over the weeks, as deadlock developed and then persisted, the delegates recalled the idea and began to see its wisdom. When Ellsworth broached the subject again, he couched Sherman's plan in more appealing terms, saying that the plan would check both political corruption in the large states and dictatorial tendencies in a band of small states.[88] The Convention debated the matter for a week.

The question of representation was then sent to the Gerry Committee, headed by Elbridge Gerry of Massachusetts. This committee's formation was a triumph for the small states. The committee was formed to examine the idea of representation in the new government, and it was packed with men in favor of equal representation for the small states: Gerry favored the small states, as did Oliver Ellsworth of Connecticut. Benjamin Franklin supported equal representation, William Paterson of New Jersey, who was, of course, for equal representation, Luther Martin of Maryland, Gunning Bedford of Deleware, George Mason of Virginia, Abraham Baldwin of Georgia, William Davie of North Carolina, and John Rutledge of South Carolina: Almost to a person, every member of the Gerry Committee was in favor of small states' rights.

The Gerry Committee decided that the lower House should be based on population, and that there should be one representative in the House for every 40,000 inhabitants. This favored the large states. The Gerry Committee also called for equal representation in the upper House, the Senate, with every state, regardless of size,

---

88   *Ibid.*

receiving an equal vote. The third proposal of the Gerry Committee was that all the money bills should originate in the House and not be subject to amendment in the upper chamber, which was another idea in favor of the large states. It would be the money bills originating in the House that helped convince Mason, and even Gerry to some extent, to support the proposals. The small-state men were willing to concede two of the three points of the Gerry Committee's recommendations, as long as there was equal representation in the Senate.

Almost immediately the Convention went from hanging in the balance to suddenly, at the opening of business on July 16, once again being a viable Convention with real hopes of success. The compromise on representation passed with a vote of five states to four, with Massachusetts divided. The deadlock was broken. In the years to come, members of the assembly would credit Roger Sherman and his Connecticut Compromise, as it came to be called, with saving the Convention. The delegates still had much to discuss—the appointment of judges, the establishment of tribunals, and the nature of the executive branch. But in August, the issue that had been lingering below the surface since the very first days of the Convention finally came out into the open: *the issue of slavery.*

The 3/5ths Compromise

There were many fault lines at the Convention: large states versus the small states, northern states versus the southern, the eastern states versus the southern, and in some ways, there was a crossover in those fault lines: the southern states, excluding Virginia, were smaller states. Georgia and South Carolina combined to represent only 5% of the population in the United States: of the 3.5 million people living in America at the time, only about 175,000 lived in those two states.

In August, once the Great Compromise had been reached, the smaller, southern states realized that if the lower House was based on population, they would be overwhelmed by the larger states in the House: Virginia could have up to 16 times more power in the lower House than Georgia. The central theme of the slave debates at the Convention was really over the issue of how to count slaves when deciding population: if the lower House was based on population, the southern states, already with smaller populations, wanted every advantage they could get. They wanted the slaves to count just as any other persons in the census, yet it was of course only in this instance that they wanted them to be considered more than just property.

In addition, even though the slave states treated slaves as property, they did not want slaves taxed as property. In short, the southern states wanted it both ways: They didn't want to consider the slaves real people, just property, except when it came to the census, but even then didn't want to pay an importation tax on slaves. They were obviously not prepared to grant slaves the full rights of citizenship, yet neither did they want to acknowledge that they were property.

To better understand what was at stake over the issue of whether slaves should be counted in the census, slaves comprised 40%

of the South's population at this time. If the delegates from South Carolina, North Carolina, and Georgia could have had their entire slave population fully counted in the census, it would have given the southern slave states a dramatic increase in the population and, ergo, more power in the lower House; it would have meant a 40% increase in their power in the House. Every delegate at the Convention knew all of these facts, knew that there were deeply held beliefs on both sides of the debate. The slave debates at the Convention would illuminate the fractures and moral conflicts already simmering beneath the surface of American society that would burst into a bloody civil war less than 100 years later.

In early August, Pierce Butler of South Carolina put a fine point on what the southern states wanted: "I contend that representation be according to the full number of inhabitants, including all the blacks." The northern states were of course never going to agree to that and instead, led by Gouvernor Morris of Pennsylvania, began insisting that as time went on and populations changed, the national legislature should be empowered "to vary representation according to the principles of wealth and number of inhabitants" and that taxation would be in proportion to representation. The northern states realized that if the slaves were included in the census for purposes of representation, what was to prevent the South from simply importing more slaves? Many of the northern delegates advocated that the slaves shouldn't be counted at all. But at minimum, the northern states drew a line in the sand that they would never give the southern slave states more political power off the shoulders of the slaves and would never allow all of them to be counted fully in the census for political power. In addition to that, the northern delegates insisted that an importation tax of $10/head would be enacted to help further discourage importation.

The slave states were furious at both ideas. William Davie of North Carolina finally exploded: "It is high time to speak out! This motion [of taxation] is meant by some gentlemen to deprive the southern states of any share of representation for their blacks! I am sure that North Carolina would never confederate on any terms that did not rate the negroes at least at 3/5ths. If the Eastern States meant therefore to exclude us altogether, the business is at an end!"

The idea of slaves counting as 3/5ths of the population for representation purposes was not in fact an idea original to the Convention. It had been proposed more than four years before in the Continental Congress that "in order to ascertain the alterations in representation that may be required from time to time by changes in the relative circumstances of the states, a census shall be taken within two years . . . all the inhabitants in the manner and according to the ratio recommended by Congress . . . rating the blacks at 3/5ths of their number."

Morris of Pennsylvania, however, refused to even accept that figure as legitimate: "I verily believe that the people of Pennsylvania will never agree to a representation of negroes. What can be desired by these states has already been proposed; that the legislature shall from time to time regulate representation according to population and wealth."

There was a growing sense inside of the Convention that after the months of work, the compromises already reached might all be in vain if a compromise was not struck regarding slaves and representation. It was Oliver Ellsworth of Connecticut who officially proposed that slaves be counted as 3/5ths in representation matters, while Butler of South Carolina would again insist that the slaves be equal to the whites in the issue of representation. Rufus King of Massachusetts replied that the issue of admitting slaves at all into the rule of representation was "a most grating circumstance. . . ." He would "never agree to let them be imported without limitation and then be represented in the National Legislature."

Morris, one of the most active speakers at the Convention, was just as adamant in his refusal to allow slaves to be counted in the census: "I move to insert 'free' before the word inhabitants. Much will depend on this point. I will never concur in upholding domestic slavery. It is the curse of heaven on the states where it prevails... Upon what principle is it that the slaves shall be computed in the representation? Are they men? Then make them citizens and let them vote. Are they property? Why then is no other property included? The houses in this city [Philadelphia] are worth more than all the wretched slaves which cover the rice swamps of South Carolina."

The debates would go back and forth, the lines hardening, passions rising. George Mason of Virginia, an owner of 200 slaves, a neighbor of Washington's, and one of the great political theorists of the day, finally stood and delivered an impassioned speech: "This infernal trade originated in the avarice of British merchants. The British government constantly checked the attempts of Virginia to put a stop to it. . . . Maryland and Virginia have already prohibited the importation of slaves expressly. North Carolina has done the same in substance. All this will be in vain if South Carolina and Georgia be at liberty to import. . . . Slavery discourages arts and manufactures. . . . They produce the most pernicious effects on manners. Every master of slaves is born a petty tyrant. They bring the judgement of heaven on a country. As nations cannot be rewarded or punished in the next world they must be in this."

Mason would hit on one of the issues regarding slaves and representation: If there was no end to importation, the southern states would, of course, continue to import them for representation purposes. Rutledge of South Carolina cooly responded to all attempts to cease importation: "If the Convention thinks that North Carolina, South Carolina, and Georgia will ever agree to the plan, unless their right to import slaves be untouched, the expectation is in vain. The people of those states will never be such fools as to give up so important an interest." Randolph of Virginia stated very clearly the dilemma facing the delegates: "By agreeing to the clause [the 3/5ths compromise], it would revolt the Quakers, the Methodists, and many others in the states having no slaves. On the other hand, two states might be lost to the Union. Let us then try the chance of a commitment."

What would ultimately come out of the slave debates at the Convention was the 3/5^{ths} compromise. The northern states finally compromised with the southern states: They would not allow a slave to count as a full person in the census; rather, a slave would be counted as three-fifths of a person. The delegates also decided that the importation of slaves would stop on January 1, 1808, and true to that compromise, on January 1, 1808, Congress outlawed the importation of slaves into the states.

It was also decided the slaves would be considered taxable property, with a $10 import tax on every slave brought into the United States. While all of this was taking place in Philadelphia, the Confederation Congress, meeting in New York City, passed the Northwest Ordinance, which did not allow any of the new states coming into the union to have any slaves in them. The ordinance, however, did allow the Fugitive Slave Act to exist in new states, meaning if a slave ran away into a free state, his master could pursue him and bring him back.

This is one issue that has always been debated, and which Progressive opponents of the Constitution have always used in an attempt to undermine the legitimacy of it: Why did the founding fathers allow slavery to continue when they could have put an end to it? Georgia and South Carolina represented only 5% of the population. Georgia really had no choice. With the Spanish in the south and the Creek Indians as a constant and present threat, Georgia had to join the union for matters of self-preservation. Perhaps if delegates such as Oliver Ellsworth, Roger Sherman, and others who were against slavery had stood firm, American history would have been different and there would never have been a civil war. But Sherman and others made a miscalculation and felt that slavery in America was going to end of its own accord, and that instead of endangering the union of all the states over the issue of slavery, they decided to compromise on the issue. Besides, the new nation simply could not afford to have a foreign power take advantage of a desperate Georgia trying to stay independent of the new republic. However, the country would pay for that compromise less than 100 years later with the deaths of hundreds of thousands of Americans in our bloody Civil War.

The Covenant Model

One of the great and overarching debates at the Constitutional Convention was that if the delegates were to create a new federal government, how could they empower it to protect individual rights? Provide for a strong national defense, and govern and standardize domestic and international commerce, yet at the same time cause that government to be limited? The government they were creating must be a self-governing government, one that would limit itself even if filled with imperfect human beings who, when given power, would naturally seek more power.

Recognizing the need for limits, the Founders sought for a government model that acknowledged an objective and realistic view of human behavior, one that established morality, justice, and law on a foundation beyond simple human wisdom and whims. The culture of Anglo-America at the Founding was no longer Puritan, but it was still informed largely by Judeo-Christian norms. The Puritan idea of a *covenant*—a voluntary, yet binding agreement between two or more parties, was still prevalent. While a covenant and a compact are similar, the primary element that distinguishes a covenant from a compact is that a compact is typically between nations or states. In a covenant, the Creator is the acknowledged arbiter between individuals: His moral law is the basis for all law. Accordingly, those participating in the covenant are accountable not only to each other, but also to God. Thievery, murder, defrauding, etc., are wrong not simply because they harm another person. They are wrong because they violate God's established moral order that predates man's ruminations. Each participant is held to the same standard, and a violation on the part of one member does not absolve another of his solemn responsibility.

The Founders derived their understanding of the covenant from their Puritan forefathers, who, in turn, had drawn it from the Bible. The covenant model appealed to Americans not only because it established a universal standard, but also because it applied to people as individuals. And while it is true that the idea of covenant was drawn from Scripture, it would be a mistake to merely view it as a religious term. At the time of the Pilgrims and the Puritans, the term often meant a legally binding contract.[89] Under a covenant, no man was at the behest of another man or group of men; instead, he answered, in his soul, to God, the Supreme Judge. Thus, a covenant could cross generations, traverse long distances and bind together people of different backgrounds; the only requirement being each

---

89   Nick Bunker, *Making Haste from Babylon: The Mayflower Pilgrims and Their World*. (New York: Vintage Books, 2010), 286.

one's willingness to participate.[90]

While the covenant could provide a spiritual bond between
the people and uphold individual liberty, the Founders were still
aware of the need for a temporal authority structure, especially
now that America was developing into the first modern republic
and not simply the Massachusetts Bay Colony or Commonwealth
of Virginia. Since no citizen would heed the law perfectly or
consistently, the people would require proper tools for maintaining
order and executing justice. Traditionally, as we have seen,
government was designed to be a master over the people, enforcing
their obedience to a state or sovereign dictating law to them.

But under a covenant, in which God was the ultimate
authority, government was added not to *dominate* the people but
to *protect* their individual liberties. The Founders designed the
mechanics of American government to preserve individual liberty,
employing several innovations for this purpose in the creation of the
Constitution.

The Puritans brought to America a deep respect for
authority, both sacred and temporal. The Founders still felt that
influence, 150 years later, as is evidenced in their writings both public
and private that often refer to concepts such as the moral law and
God's providence. The Puritans heeded the voice of their leaders
and considered it a solemn responsibility to obey them. However,
the Puritans' ultimate authority was the written Word of God;
this was the standard against which they judged the merit of their

---

90   Kirk, 289.

leaders.[91] The Bible, much like the common law, was universally available and applied equally to every member of society. It is, of course, the translation of the Bible into vernacular languages that has made it more accessible and "democratized" the Scriptures. The most significant English translations were made by John Wycliffe, and then William Tyndale, as they would set the wheels in motion for the American Revolution. But unlike the common law, the Bible was a concrete document, accessible and easily referenced. It was everyman's tool, providing a standard for his neighbor's behavior as well as his own.

This typically American passion for recorded law intensified during the Revolutionary era, when the British Parliament sought to interpret law on behalf of the colonists, thus abusing the relationship of trust that had once existed between England and the colonies. For this reason, the delegates to the Philadelphia Convention were determined to record the law in such a way as to make it immediately accessible to all Americans. The delegates achieved this goal by embodying that law in a single document, the Constitution, which could be reproduced and distributed according to need.

At the time of the Founding, a written constitution was unusual. In many countries, the law had always been associated with the individual or group in power rather than in a code. Even Great Britain, with its comparably sophisticated political development, lacked one specific, codified document specifying the

---

91   Paul Johnson, *A History of the American People* (New York: HarperCollins, 1997), 40.

limits of state power.[92] But the United States Constitution, placing explicit boundaries on the government, provided for the exercise of individual liberty to an extent never seen before.

A second and more complex innovation instituted by the Founders was the process of *ratification*. At the beginning of the Constitutional Convention, the delegates had agreed to hold all proceedings in secret. Once they realized that they were going to form a new government rather than revise the Articles, the members knew that they would have to submit their plan to the people of each state for approval. But in what manner should it be presented? Should the decision lie in the hands of the state legislatures, whose very power was threatened by the Constitution? Or should it be given to state conventions formed by the people, as the Virginia Plan had prescribed?

During the Constitutional Convention, the delegates had first addressed this question by discussing the number of states needed to ratify the Constitution. At the time, some suggested that all 13 states ought to agree before the document became law. Supporters of the Virginia Plan knew that only a miracle would make all 13 states unite on this issue. Nathaniel Gorham of Massachusetts pointed out that requiring unanimity would empower one or two states to effectively cancel the votes of the rest. Rhode Island, after all, was sure to dissent, because it never cooperated on anything. Must that rogue state be allowed to decide the fate of the other 12?[93]

Pierce Butler of South Carolina, who "revolted at the idea,

---

92   Kirk, 416.
93   Bowen, 229.

that one or two States should restrain the rest from consulting their safety," declared that nine states would be adequate for ratification.[94] James Wilson of Pennsylvania agreed, assuring the more doubtful members that no state refusing to ratify would be bound by the Constitution. After several more hours of debate, the delegates finally agreed that nine states would be sufficient.

Now the assembly took up again the question of whether the state legislatures or special conventions should vote on the Constitution. The people, said James Madison of Virginia, are "the fountain of all power;" it was their right and responsibility to deliberate directly on the structure of their own government. The state legislatures, after all, would never favor a plan that decreased their power. Nathaniel Gorham of Massachusetts agreed. If the legislatures do not reject the plan outright, he suggested, they will delay the question indefinitely "by artfully pressing a variety of little businesses."[95]

The delegates, of course, realized that more was at stake in this debate than simply securing approval of the Constitution. To grant the power of ratification to the states would be a tacit confirmation of state sovereignty. Such a gesture, insisted Madison, would violate the very definition of a constitution. "I consider the difference between a system founded on the [state] legislatures only, and one founded on the people," he declared, "to be the true difference between a league or treaty and a constitution."[96] George Mason of Virginia agreed. Leaving ratification to the state assemblies, he explained, would set a dangerous precedent. Even

---

94   *Debates in the Federal Convention of 1787*, recorded by James Madison, August 30.
95   Bowen, 228.
96   *Ibid.*, 225.

if the legislatures were to approve the Constitution, "succeeding Legislatures having equal authority could undo the acts of their predecessors; the National Government would [then] stand in each State on the weak and tottering foundation of an Act of Assembly."[97]

Despite these persuasive speeches, the controversy continued for several days, escalating to such an extent that it began to revive arguments that had long lain silent in the House. Various members began to object to the Convention's previous decisions on the balance of national power, the mode of election for federal officials, and the process of making amendments. Individual delegates declared that the current draft of the Constitution contained so many faults that they could not, in good conscience, sign it. George Mason even suggested that another convention be called to resolve the remaining difficulties.

The thought of a second convention was nauseating to a great many delegates. Determined to bring their present work to fruition, the members effectively ignored that suggestion and instead devised a compromise. State conventions called in the individual states would oversee the process of ratification, they decided, on the condition that the states be allowed to propose amendments to the Constitution.

While this compromise satisfied most members of the Convention, they knew a greater battle lay ahead in persuading the entire nation to approve their plan. With this in mind, they agreed to prepare a letter to the public to accompany the printing

---

97   Ketcham, 128.

of the Constitution. "We have now the honor," the letter began, "to submit to the consideration of the United States assembled, that Constitution which has appeared to us the most advisable." Aware of the opposition they faced, the Founders spoke in the letter cautiously, yet sincerely: "In all our deliberations ... we have kept steadily in our view, that which appears to us the greatest interest of every true American, the consolidation of our union. . . . This important consideration, seriously and deeply impressed on our minds, led each State in the Convention to be less rigid on points of inferior magnitude." The paragraph closed with a tenor more hopeful than certain: "[T]hus the Constitution, which we now present, is the result of a spirit of amity, and of that mutual deference and concession which the peculiarity of our political situation rendered indispensable."[98]

"We the People of the United States . . . "

By the beginning of September, the debates were resolved among the delegates, and it was time to draft the final Constitution. William Samuel Johnson from Connecticut was made the chairman of the drafting committee, the Committee of Style. Alexander Hamilton of New York was also chosen, having returned to the Convention. James Madison, Rufus King of Massachusetts, along with Gouverneur Morris of Pennsylvania, comprised the rest of the committee. Morris was chosen by the committee to be the penman of the Constitution, much like Thomas Jefferson had been the

---

98   Madison Debates, September 12.

penman of the Declaration of Independence.

The initial draft went to the floor and was debated, then sent back to Morris for the rewrites. Morris felt that to be a truly great writer of history one must be a reader of Shakespeare; there must be muscle to one's writing, but at the same time, symmetry and grace. He felt very strongly that his writing must be graceful, and it is he who came up with the phrase: "We the people of the United States, in order to form a more perfect union. . . ." Morris would always be proud of the work he had done on the Constitution, and many, including Madison, recognized Morris for the work he had done in pulling together these ideas and putting them into a cohesive form while adding a certain beauty to the writing.

The final draft of the Constitution went to the floor of the Convention on September 17, 1787. There were some surprises that morning. Elbridge Gerry of Massachusetts decided he could not sign the document: "From the collision of these in opposing and resisting the Constitution, confusion is greatly to be feared. I think it necessary, for this and other reasons, that the plan should have been proposed in a more mediating shape, in order to abate the heat and opposition of parties. As it has been passed by the Convention, I am persuaded it will have a contrary effect."

George Mason, also part of the Gerry committee who came up with the compromises that allowed the Convention to move forward, also refused to sign. But perhaps the greatest surprise was that Edmund Randolph, who introduced the Virginia Plan, refused to sign the document. Benjamin Franklin told Randolph that morning that if he did not sign the document that he himself proposed, and the public found out, it would not look right. Yet Randolph refused to sign for several reasons. He felt there wasn't enough power in the lower House; that the people were not going to be represented well enough in the new government unless there were more representatives in the House of Representatives. Washington spoke for only the second time at the Convention, and he supported the idea that the ratio of representation to population should be reduced from 1 to 40,000 to 1 to 30,000, thereby increasing the number of representatives in the House. Washington was clearly trying to bring Randolph on board to sign the document, but still Randolph refused. However, 39 of the original 55 delegates to the Convention signed the Constitution that day in Philadelphia.

As the last of the delegates were signing the document, Madison recounted that Franklin looked toward the chair Washington had been sitting in that summer. On the back of it a rising sun had been painted. Franklin commented: "I have said here often and often in the source of the session, and the vicissitudes of my hopes and fears as to its issues, looked at that behind the President without being able to tell whether it was rising or setting: but now at length I have the happiness to know that it is a rising and not a setting sun." As he left the state house that day, a woman asked Franklin, "Well Doctor, what have we got: a republic or a monarchy?" Franklin replied: "A republic, if you can keep it."

CHAPTER EIGHT

The Constitution and the American Citizen

———————◆———————

"The fate of . . . America may depend on this: Have they said, we the States?... If they had, this [system] would be a confederation: It is otherwise most clearly a consolidated government. The question turns, Sir, on that poor little thing—the expression, *We the people...*"[99]

As he addressed the Virginia Ratifying Convention in the spring of 1788, statesman Patrick Henry spoke for many as he voiced his objections to the new Constitution. "Here is a revolution as radical as that which separated us from Great Britain," he said, referring to the consolidation of power in the national government. "It is as radical, if in this transition our rights and privileges are endangered, and the sovereignty of the States be relinquished: And cannot we plainly see, that this is actually the case?"[100]

When the delegates to the Constitutional Convention signed

---

99   Patrick Henry to the Virginia Ratifying Convention, June 5, 1788. Ralph Ketcham, ed., *The Anti-Federalist Papers and the Constitutional Convention Debates* (New York: Mentor, 1986), 199.
100   *Ibid.*, 199, 200.

the Constitution, they were fully aware that their job was only half done. Now, they faced the daunting challenge of persuading their constituents to approve the document. The task was formidable: The public, by and large, was shocked by the Constitution. After all, they had sent representatives to Philadelphia to revise the Articles, not to devise an entirely new system. In addition, as Patrick Henry noted, the Constitution prescribed a national government that operated upon the people directly, instead of governing them through the state legislatures. Such a prospect was frightening: How could a single system govern America's vast land and large population without turning tyrannical?

Returning to their home states, the delegates begged the public not to be alarmed. "Hearken not to the voice which petulantly tells you that the form of government recommended for your adoption is a novelty in the political world," pled Alexander Hamilton to the people of New York. "No, my countrymen, shut your ears against this unhallowed language." Despite Hamilton's earnest words, the delegates could not ignore the fact that their plan *was* new. The form of government prescribed in the Constitution *was* without precedent, but it was built upon a foundation composed not only of elements from past civilizations but also of lessons gleaned from America's unique colonial experience.

Lessons from the Past

"We have heard," wrote Alexander Hamilton in 1787, "of the impious doctrine in the old world that the people were made for kings, not kings for the people. Is this same doctrine to be revived in the new? . . . Let us not forget," he warned, "that the public good, the real welfare of the great body of the people, is the supreme object to be pursued; and that no form of Government whatever, has any other value, than as it may be fitted for the attainment of this object."[101]

The delegates who gathered at the Constitutional Convention knew that, in great civilizations of the past, people had constructed their governments according to the needs of the state, rather than the needs of the people themselves. Such designs were often secular manifestations of a given culture's religion. In ancient Rome, for example, the supremacy of the state reflected the people's pantheistic or pagan beliefs. Romans believed that the universe was ruled by a host of gods and goddesses, each of whom controlled a different aspect of nature or daily life. People lived in perpetual fear of offending the gods and expended much energy in trying to appease them by building temples, performing rituals, and offering sacrifices. The government or state was thought to be a quasi-divine mediator between the people and the gods, and as such required the obedience and devotion of its subjects. In the imperial age, some Roman emperors even demanded to be worshipped as gods themselves. Because the state had authority to interpret divine favor or displeasure, citizens were compelled to serve the government for their own good. In this type of society, the individual was always

---

101   James Madison, *Federalist No. 45,* The Federalist Papers, ed. Garry Wills (New York: Bantam Books, 1982), 233.

defined by his relationship to the state.[102] Man was for the state; the state was not for the man.

In America, the situation was radically different. In addition to their Judeo-Christian heritage, which could never countenance worship of the state, the people of the Founding generation had inherited from their Puritan forefathers a strong sense of mission: They believed that they were a people called of God to establish a righteous and free nation on earth. The American individual was to be defined not by his relationship to the state, but by his relationship to *God*. Man needed no earthly mediator, for Christ had already provided direct access to the Father. God had created man in His image; therefore, every individual has intrinsic value and worth.

These concepts profoundly influenced the proceedings at the Federal Convention, now known as the Constitutional Convention. The Founders believed that a free society was built on the foundation of individual rights and the needs of the individual—not the wishes of the state. But was this not contradictory? How were they to devise a government that was strong enough to maintain order but was limited in such a way as not to endanger individual liberty?

Faced with such questions, the Founding Fathers were forced to draw deeply upon their religious beliefs. These beliefs were woven into the fabric of the culture, whether a given individual was an orthodox Christian or not. Many believed the Biblical account that God created man in His image and endowed him with a right to dignity and freedom. Therefore, because all men bear God's

---

102   M. Stanton Evans, *The Theme is Freedom: Religion, Politics, and the American Tradition* (Washington, DC: Regnery, 1994), 135-136.

image, all are equal: No man has a right to remove or violate the liberty of another. The issue of slavery would, of course, highlight the human flaw present in many of us: *knowing what is right, yet lacking the courage to act upon it.* While the Founders fundamentally believed in innate human dignity, and many were quite vocal in their condemnation of slavery, their compromises revealed inconsistencies in their beliefs and logic. Despite their shortcomings, the Founders wrestled with the question: "What is the purpose of government?" If man derived his liberty from God and was accountable to Him for his actions, what need did an earthly government fulfill?

The conviction that influenced the Founders' political actions perhaps more than any other was the certainty that human nature is inherently corrupt. Man, they believed, had been incapable of sustained good ever since his rejection of God in the Garden of Eden. This principle had been firmly entrenched in American culture from the days of the first Puritan settlers. Consequently, Americans had always been highly suspicious of "Utopian speculations" or of any theory that relied exclusively upon man's goodness.[103]

For this reason, many of the Founders were skeptical of the idea of a confederacy. "Does anyone really believe," asked Hamilton, "that 13 sovereign states can dwell together peacefully?" To do so "would be to forget that men are ambitious, vindictive, and rapacious. To look for a continuation of harmony between a number of independent unconnected sovereignties . . . would be to disregard the uniform course of human events, and to set at defiance

---

103   Alexander Hamilton, *Federalist No. 6*, Federalist Papers, 21.

the accumulated experience of ages."[104] Since men could not be entirely trusted to act justly toward one another, they required an authority or government to hold them accountable to the law. Thus, government was a good thing, for it maintained order in society, enabling men to exercise their freedoms responsibly.

However, the Founders knew too well from history that governments, because they consisted of men, could be just as corrupt as the people under them. In many ways, rulers had a capacity for greater evil than ordinary men. Armed with the power of the state and the arrogance provoked by achieving that power, they could easily abuse and violate the liberties of their subjects.

It was this problem of the state's abuse of power that attracted the interest of writers and thinkers in the era preceding the Enlightenment. As they grew increasingly disgusted with European monarchies, these theorists began to seek an ideal form of government: one that honored individual rights. There was a great debate as to the right form of government that brought order to society. Thomas Hobbes (1588-1679), on the one hand, a 17th-century British philosopher, was skeptical of man's ability to exercise freedom properly. In his treatise, *The Leviathan* (1660), Hobbes portrays government as a necessary evil, preferable only to the evil of unrestrained men. Men are motivated only by selfish interests, Hobbes says; if left to their own devices, men will wrong and kill each other. The only power strong enough to restrain man's wickedness is fear. Therefore, the only type of government able to

---

104   *Ibid.*, 22.

maintain an orderly society is an absolute monarchy.[105]

On the other hand, later theorists had a more optimistic attitude toward the human race. John Locke (1632-1704), a British academic whose work heavily influenced the Founders' thinking, believed that man was capable of exercising his freedoms responsibly. He attempted to refute Hobbes in his *Two Treatises of Government* (1690), arguing that man must fully appreciate his own inherent liberties before he can discover a superior form of government. "To understand the Political Power right, and derive it from its Original," wrote Locke, "we must consider what State all Men are naturally in, and that is, a *State of perfect Freedom* to order their Actions, and dispose of their Possessions, and Persons as they think fit, within the bounds of the Law of Nature. . . ."[106]

However, Locke emphasized that this "State of Liberty" did not equal a "State of License." Man's right to life, liberty, and property never entitled him to violate the rights of another. In order to ensure the equal protection of all, wrote Locke, men come together in mutual agreement to form a community, a "just association." The privilege of belonging to this community comes with a price: Each individual must voluntarily surrender his personal sovereignty to the sovereignty of the people as a whole. This sacrificial action transforms a group of individuals into a "civil society." The individual, said Locke, "authorizes the Society, [or] the Legislative thereof to make Laws for him as the publick good of the

---

105   Kirk, 270.
106   John Locke, *Two Treatises of Government*, ed. Peter Laslett (New York: Cambridge University, 1960), 309.

Society shall require; to the Execution whereof, his own assistance (as to his own Decrees) is due.[107] The voluntary quality of this pact is significant: No man is constrained to join the community, but once he has chosen to enter it, he is bound to support and serve the society.

The Founding Fathers appreciated Locke's regard for natural law, individual rights, and popular sovereignty. But while Locke's theory proved useful to them on an intellectual level, it lacked both the spirituality and practicality so characteristic of American thought. First, Locke's model bound together a community merely on the basis of self-interest. Though the Founders fully comprehended the power of self-interest upon a people's actions, they recognized that it did not always lead them to do what was right. A truly free society, they believed, must engage an individual's moral interest as well as his more human aspirations.

Second, Locke's theory was of limited practicality because it failed to explain how a people could trust themselves to govern justly and treat every citizen equally. The Founders were right to be concerned, because such a theory could lead to the tyranny of a majority acting on impulse and with no concern for the moral law. Even as they wrote the Constitution, a revolution was developing in France that would take just such a course, spurred on by Jean-Jacques Rousseau's radical notion of the Social Contract that argued blatantly that the "general will" of the majority is what should govern a nation. In this case, the French lower classes, oppressed for many

---

107   *Ibid.*, 368-369.

years under a corrupt monarchy and ruling class, eagerly seized upon Enlightenment theories that advocated equality and individual rights—and anyone in their way would be mowed down, *literally*. Making matters worse, the French in the radical stage of their revolution suffered under the misconception that certain types of authority, rather than human beings, are evil. They were convinced that, by simply transferring power from the king to the people, they could solve all social ills and restore justice to the land.[108] They did not believe that humanity is inherently corrupt. The bloody results of the French Revolution soon revealed their error and demonstrated that *all* temporal power, not just the power of the king, must be restricted.

The Ratification Battles

In the anxious yet productive months that followed the signing of the Constitution, as state conventions deliberated over the new plan, the people gradually came to see the wisdom not only of the Constitution but also of the method of its ratification. By design, ratification conventions were temporary bodies, consolidating the people's authority for the specific purpose of considering the Constitution. After their decisions were made, the conventions would dissolve. Thus, in the future, no official or legislative body would be able to challenge the established Constitution; the people had made their choice, and only they could alter it.

The process of ratification lasted nearly two and a half

---

108   Evans, 253.

years. The delegates from the Convention, especially those who had supported the Virginia Plan, lobbied vigorously in their home states for acceptance of the Constitution. In December of 1787, Delaware became the first state to ratify the Constitution, earning itself the nickname "The First State." Pennsylvania and New Jersey also ratified in December, followed by Georgia and Connecticut in January of 1788.

In Massachusetts, Samuel Adams played a large role in the ratification of the Constitution. He felt, along with Mason and others, that the Constitution must have a bill of rights attached to the document to protect the rights of individual citizens against any kind of abuse from the new government. When it appeared that the ratification of the Constitution in Massachusetts was in doubt, it was Adams, despite his doubts, who persuaded John Hancock, then Governor of the state, to appear at the ratifying convention to endorse the Constitution—a move that ensured its eventual ratification.

Rhode Island, which did not send any delegates to the Convention, decided to hold a unique ratification convention: It held a town hall meeting in which individual citizens had a vote. It wasn't like an actual ratification convention where delegates were elected to go to. Every male citizen had the right to vote on the ratifying of the Constitution. With this unique approach and its reputation as "Rogue Island," it was hardly a surprise that the Constitution ratification was defeated overwhelmingly, with more than 2,000 votes against, and only about 200 in favor.

Yet by the late spring of 1788, eight states had ratified the

Constitution. Nine were needed for total ratification. Virginia and New York, two states with very large and powerful Anti-Federalist contingents, scheduled their ratification conventions for the summer of 1788. The Anti-Federalists in New York felt that if their allies in Virginia could defeat the ratification of the Constitution, they would be successful as well. And if those two large and influential states could defeat the ratification, perhaps the other two states, New Hampshire and North Carolina would follow their lead.

Attention turned to Virginia, considered by many to be the Anti-Federalists' greatest hope. There were numerous national political giants at the Virginia ratification debates. The Anti-Federalists, led by Patrick Henry, were bolstered by Benjamin Harrison, a signer of the Declaration of Independence, Richard Henry Lee, another signer of the Declaration, and George Mason, one of the most respected politicians in the country at the time. The Federalist forces were led by James Madison, who was joined by John Marshall, a future Supreme Court Chief Justice. Edmund Randolph was also present, but because he had refused to sign the Constitution in Philadelphia, no one was sure what he would do.

Patrick Henry came out swinging in the debates. "Whither has the spirit of America gone, whither has the genius of America fled?" he asked. "We drew the spirit of liberty from our British ancestors but now, sir, the American spirit, assisted by the ropes and chains of consolidation, is about to convert this country into a powerful and mighty empire. What can avail your specious and imaginary balances, your rope dancing, your chain rattling, ridiculous ideal, checks and contrivances?" Henry was furious with the new Constitution. He had been elected as a delegate to the Federal Convention but refused to go, saying he "smelt a rat."

To add to the drama of it at all, there was an "X factor": Because the Kentucky territory was considered part of Virginia at the time, there were 14 Kentuckians present, colorful figures who appeared at the ratification convention with their braces of pistols and sabers at their sides, having ridden through Indian country to get to the convention. Henry, realizing that 14 votes could decide which direction the convention would go, appealed to the fears of the Kentuckians, claiming that the United States under the new Constitution would be giving away their rights to the Mississippi River to Spain.[109]

Henry, known for his passionate eloquence, lashed out in defense of states' rights. "Who authorizes gentlemen to speak the language of 'We, the people,' instead of 'We, the states'?" he demanded once during a *seven-hour* speech. "The people gave them no power to use their name."[110]

In the midst of the convention debates, Randolph began defending the Constitution, an odd twist of events for someone who refused to sign the document in Philadelphia. Henry responded to Randolph's defense of the Constitution: "The gentleman's alteration of opinion is very strange and unaccountable. Did he not tell us that

---

109   Patrick Henry, *Foreign Wars, Civil Wars, and Indian Wars — Three Bugbears*; Virginia Ratification convention, June 5, 7, and 9, 1788. https://constitution.org/afp/borden04.htm (accessed October 15, 2019).
110   Bowen, 298.

he withheld his signature? He was not then led by the illumined, the illustrious few. What alterations have a few months brought about! Something extraordinary must have operated so great a change in his opinions."

Randolph replied: "If our friendship must fall, let it fall like Lucifer, never to rise again. He has accused me of inconsistency, Sir. If I do not stand on the bottom of integrity and pure love of Virginia as much as those who can be most clamorous, I wish to resign my existence." Debate grew so heated that James Madison, after a particularly fierce altercation with Henry, took to his bed for three days.[111] However, when it came time for the final vote, the Constitution was ratified by Virginia, 89-79 in June of 1788, though Henry and Mason, like Samuel Adams, strongly recommended a Bill of Rights be attached to the Constitution.

Virginia had hoped for the honor of being the ninth and final state needed for the ratification of the Constitution. However, four days before, New Hampshire had ratified the Constitution, thereby becoming the ninth and final state needed. The ratification in Virginia caused the Anti-Federalist resistance in New York to collapse, though the Constitution would be approved by only three votes, and one month after Virginia ratified, New York followed suit. North Carolina did not ratify until the next year, on November 21, 1789. Eventually, even Rhode Island was persuaded that being outside of the Union was not in its best interests, and it ratified on May 29, 1790.

As news of the final ratification of the Constitution spread,

---

111   *Ibid.*, 300.

the country erupted into joy. In each state, people marched in parades, ran alongside marching bands, and sang songs written for the occasion. Coastal towns christened new ships with names such as *Union, Federal Constitution* and *Rising Sun.*[112] The Constitutional Convention had, in effect, won its own revolution. America, having already waged a war of musket and cannon, had triumphed in a more unique national struggle. De Tocqueville later described this achievement in his own words:

> [W]hat is new in the history of societies is to see a great people, warned by its legislators that the wheels of the government are stopping, turn its regard on itself without haste and fear, sound the depth of the ill, contain itself for two entire years in order to discover the remedy at leisure, and when the remedy is pointed out, submit voluntarily to it without its costing humanity one tear or drop of blood.[113]

---

112   *Ibid.*, 306-308.
113   de Tocqueville, 106.

CHAPTER NINE
Rights Enumerated

———————◆———————

In the closing days of the Constitutional Convention, George Mason, mindful of the fact that the new Constitution would result in a more powerful federal government, proposed a clearly stated bill of individual rights. In the face of concentrated power, Mason believed strongly that a line must be drawn, delineating where the government powers ended and the rights of the individual began.

The idea of enumerated individual rights was nothing new for Mason. Just over 10 years before, in 1776, Mason had authored most of the Virginia Declaration of Rights and the state constitution at a convention called specifically to draft those documents. Joining him on the drafting committee for the declaration of rights was a young 25 year old by the name of James Madison, who, while new to politics and didn't play a significant role at the Virginia convention, would add an important clause which would state the right to the "free exercise of religion."[114] The final draft of the Virginia Declaration of Rights included 16 clauses, with statements such as, "all men are by nature equally free and independent," and "all power is vested in, and consequently derived from the People," and "the freedom of the Press is one of the great bulwarks of liberty," and that there was to be a well-regulated militia.

Far from being unique, the Virginia Declaration of Rights was really just the latest in a long line of documents stretching over six centuries that were part of the Anglo-American tradition of declaring rights. The beginning was, in many ways, the Magna Carta, where on the meadows of Runnymede, the barons, "sword in hand," obtained from King John the rights they demanded, including that King John could not jail, tax or otherwise molest or abuse the lords and barons without following the law and without jury trials, nor could he by fiat decide who would be appointed bishops of the church.

Roughly four centuries later, Parliament would confront King Charles I over his behavior regarding the funding of the Thirty Years' War. Frustrated by Parliament's refusal to give him the monies he demanded for the war efforts, Charles began "forcing loans" from the nobility, imprisoning those who did not comply, quartering troops in the homes of private citizens, and placing large sections of England under martial law. In response to these actions, Parliament insisted upon a document that would restrict the king's actions and prevent him from infringing upon the rights of Englishmen. In other

---

114   John J. Patrick, *The Bill of Rights; A History in Documents* (New York: Oxford University Press, 2003), 58.

words, English monarchs had to be reminded yet again that long ago they had lost their ability to rule as absolute monarchs. Despite Charles' extreme reluctance to sign the document, in the face of a unified House of Commons and Lords, he relented, and on June 7, 1628, he assented to the Petition of Right which, among other things, states "no person should be compelled to make any loans to the king against his will" that "no free person would be imprisoned without cause" nor would private citizens any longer be compelled to house soldiers.

Yet Charles I refused to live by the Petition of Right and provoked the English Civil War. The Parliament, led by Oliver Cromwell, eventually defeated him and ultimately beheaded him. Cromwell established a commonwealth, but the tradition of the monarchy was too strong in England, and eventually the Stuart dynasty would return to power, with Charles II assuming his father's place. Charles II was more circumspect than his father, but nevertheless tried to exercise absolute power himself. He managed not to get himself overthrown or executed, passing the crown to his younger brother, James II, upon his death. James II, unfortunately, behaved more like his father than his brother and also provoked a revolution against himself, known as the Glorious Revolution. Among other things, he abused the Protestants of England, which led to his downfall. These forces, determined to have Parliamentary supremacy, overthrew James without violence and forced him to flee to France. Parliament invited the Dutch Prince, William of Orange, nephew to Charles I, and his wife, Mary, the daughter of James II and James' heir, to take up the English throne. But the crown came with a price: Parliament passed yet another declaration of rights, the Bill of Rights in 1689, to address the abuses of James II. Determined to prevent more monarchical abuse, Parliament presented to the newly installed King William III and Queen Mary II their declaration of rights, which included the right of free elections for the House of Commons, the right of Parliament to meet regularly, no taxes without the assent of Parliament, that Protestants had the right to bear arms for self-defense, and that there were to be no excessive bails or cruel and unusual punishments. This bill was not a *suggestion* to William and Mary, but a *requirement* for their accession to the throne. The document also listed Parliament's grievances against James II; it is not hard to see how it influenced Thomas Jefferson in his writing of our Declaration of Independence. The 1689 Bill of Rights became one of the most important documents of the uncodified British constitution.

The Founders were familiar with these documents, Mason literally taking word for word some lines from the 1689 Bill of Rights and Hamilton referring to both the Petition of Right and the 1689 Bill of Rights in *Federalist 84*. But at the Constitutional Convention, the idea that the American republic needed an actual bill of rights was dismissed by Hamilton and Madison. Their dismissal was clearly not because of a disbelief in individual rights but because they believed strongly that these rights were inherent throughout the Constitution, that the document itself "in every rational sense, and to every useful purpose, [was] a bill of rights" by declaring and specifying the "political privileges of the citizens in the structure and administration of the government."

It is important to note that Madison and Hamilton did not believe that the best way to guard individual rights was by creating a document listing them. In fact, Hamilton was concerned that in so doing, any rights left off such a list might be construed to not be a right at all. He wrote in *Federalist 84*, "I go further, and affirm that bills of rights, in the sense and to the extent in which they are contended for, are not only unnecessary in the proposed Constitution, but would even be dangerous"[115] "Why should it be said that the liberty of the press shall not be restrained, when no power is given by which restrictions may be imposed?"[116] Hamilton thus argued that no bill of individual rights is needed when, in fact, the new national government had no right or power to encroach upon the rights protected in the first place.

This is an important point to stress. Jefferson penned the words in the Declaration of Independence that "to secure these rights, Governments are instituted among Men, deriving their just powers from the consent of the governed." Governments were to *secure* rights; not *give* rights, and certainly take none of them away. To do so would be the antithesis of why government existed in the first place. So in Hamilton's reasoning, why was there a need for a document of *stated* rights when in fact government was never given the power to dictate what rights should or should not exist.

---

115   Alexander Hamilton, John Jay and James Madison. *The Federalist*, ed. George W. Carey and James McClellan. (Indianapolis: Liberty Fund, 2001), 445.
116   *Ibid.*

Ultimately Madison and Hamilton believed that the greatest ensurer of rights in the face of the power of the state was in fact the *machinery* of a constitutional republic: the diffusion of power via the separation of powers throughout the federal and state governments. If power were not concentrated but instead *separated* between the executive, legislative, and judicial branches, and furthermore, between the federal and the states via the concept of federalism, then government would remain limited in size and scope—kept in check and unable to infringe on individual rights.

Yet Mason was unconvinced by these arguments. He insisted that a Bill of Rights must be stated clearly to avoid any confusion on the limits of government power. While it was true the separation of powers and machinery of the republic being proposed would safeguard individual rights, Mason insisted on further guards, even more defenses against government encroachment. In the closing days of the Federal Convention, Mason proposed a committee to draft a bill of rights. While supported by Elbridge Gerry, Mason's proposal was overwhelmingly voted down. The following day, it was said, "Mason scowled as he studied the printed draft of the Constitution prepared by the Committee of Style. He turned the draft over and started to write on the back his 'Objections to this Constitution of Government.' His main objection, was of course, 'There is no declaration of rights.'"[117]

This disagreement over a Bill of Rights would be one of the main sticking points for the Anti-Federalists during the ratification

---

117   Patrick, 64.

battles. Madison realized that only a Bill of Rights would unite those still left with questions about the new Union. Perhaps still recovering from the bruising ratification battle in Virginia only a few short months before, Madison wrote Thomas Jefferson in October of 1788 about his change of heart regarding the need for a Bill of Rights: "[A]mong the advocates for the Constitution, there are some who wish for further guards to public liberty & individual rights. As far as these may consist of a constitutional declaration of the most essential rights, it is probable they will be added; though there are many who think such addition unnecessary, and not a few who think it misplaced in such a Constitution... My own opinion has always been in favor of a bill of rights; provided it be so framed as not to imply powers not meant to be included in the enumeration." While Madison "whitewashed" to a certain extent his resistance to Mason's idea of a Bill of Rights just over a year before in Philadelphia, after the bruising ratification battles, Madison was now firmly in favor of one.

When the first Congress met under the new constitutional form of government, the various states were encouraged to send recommendations for the proposed Bill of Rights. They responded enthusiastically with 189 suggestions.[118] The newly elected Representative Madison was tasked with culling through the long list, and he ultimately collected 17 of the suggestions as the beginning framework for a Bill of Rights. Congress, after debate in both chambers, eventually narrowed that list to 12 rights, and President

---

118   W. Cleon Skousen, *The Making of America: The Substance and Meaning of the Constitution* (Washington, DC: The National Center for Constitutional Studies, 1985), 226.

Washington sent them to the states for ratification in October of 1789. On December 15, 1791, Virginia was the 10th of 14 states (Vermont having joined the United States as the 14th state earlier in 1791) to approve 10 of the 12 amendments, thereby giving us our Bill of Rights.

A Uniquely American Bill of Rights

Our republic's Bill of Rights is both uniquely American and yet fully in the tradition of previous declarations of rights. Drawn from the rich English traditions of stated and declared individual rights throughout the centuries, it was heavily influenced by our Founders' experiences before and during the American Revolution. It is not hard to discern the handiwork of Madison and Mason in the 10 amendments which compose the Bill of Rights. With Madison tasked with compiling the rights suggested, freedom of religion is in the very first amendment, as is the freedom of the press. While Mason's 13th clause in the Virginia Declaration of Rights declared the need for a well-regulated militia, it is the Second Amendment in our Bill of Rights.

While heavily influenced by previous declarations of rights, our Bill of Rights is unique in that it shows how the Founders were impacted by their recent struggle for independence from the British Empire. Take for example the establishment of the Second Amendment. Some today argue that it was adopted only because the Founders were aware of a need to establish a military force to protect against foreign powers. What should be remembered is that as citizens of the British Empire, seeking a restoration and reformation of their rights, the Founders believed that the last defense of human rights, to property, speech, liberty, and freedom, rested in the ability to resist by force. So a well-equipped military force, yes, but one that is made up of free citizens who have a right to defend themselves from all threats, including threats emanating from those who purport to govern the republic. When all rhetoric and appeals are exhausted, as theirs were with King George III and Parliament, the Founders took the next natural step: armed resistance to tyranny. And this has been true throughout human history and across all cultures: In the face of overweening intrusion and abuse of rights by a domineering state, human beings must have recourse to defend their rights, by force if need be, and the Founders intended to have an armed citizenry, then and now.

The Third Amendment regarding the quartering of soldiers in private homes was in direct response to the Quartering Act of 1765, in which the British government forced the citizens of Boston to house British soldiers. It is also in the tradition of the Petition of Right of 1628 in which Parliament forbade Charles I from doing exactly the same thing. And while the Fourth Amendment is to protect us today against unreasonable searches, it is in direct response to the British writs of assistance in the 1760s. Frustrated by the rampant smuggling taking place in Boston, with John Hancock prominent among the smugglers, the writs gave British customs agents the right to, at any time, without warning, search private property and warehouses, while looking for smuggled goods. James

Otis, a lawyer and one of the most forceful voices for American rights in Boston during the 1760s, was one of the leading figures in fighting the writs. John Adams described the moment in the winter of 1761 when Otis stood in front of the superior court judges and argued that the writs violated the natural rights of all Englishmen. Adams, crammed into the gallery above with his fellow Bostonians, wrote that it was that very moment of Otis' defense, in which Otis was a "flame unto himself," that "the child independence was born."

The Seventh Amendment was in many ways a response to the Admiralty Courts, in which the American colonists were to be judged before a British court, not a jury of peers, and tried in a setting, Nova Scotia, not on American shores. It can be argued that the Ninth and Tenth Amendments were a nod to Hamilton and Mason respectively. The Ninth addresses Hamilton's fears and concerns that somehow any rights not enumerated in the Constitution were to be understood as nonexistent: the Ninth "specifically roots the Constitution in a natural rights tradition that says we are born with more rights than any constitution could ever list or specify."[119] The Tenth Amendment left to the states all rights and powers not specifically enumerated and given to the federal government—rights and powers which were few in number. This was, of course, Mason and all Anti-Federalists' great fear: that a powerful national government would eventually give itself more power over time, compelling the various states to surrender theirs. We know today that the Tenth is almost completely ignored, as is the concept of federalism, in that the federal government has taken power

---

119   Brian Doherty. *Radicals for Capitalism: A Freewheeling History of the Modern American Libertarian Movement* (New York City: Public Affairs, 2007), 28.

away from the states over the last century, leaving the states in a far weaker position inside the republic than the Founders ever intended.

A Last Bulwark Against the State

While Hamilton (and to a certain extent, Madison) was correct in arguing that it was the machinery of a republic that stood as the greatest defense of individual rights, over the last century, much of the machinery has been removed: from the states losing much of their power to Washington, DC, to the direct election of Senators via the 17th Amendment, to the Supreme Court undercutting and hollowing out much of the 10th Amendment. With the removal of some of the separation of powers and a consolidation of power in Washington, DC, the question now remains as to what we truly believe about individual rights and where they come from. As more and more Americans have looked to government as the giver of many things, as the solution to all problems, this mindset has allowed government to grow and become more invasive. To a certain extent, most have hardly noticed the abuse of their rights, so long as there is an illusion of peace and prosperity and needs are taken care of. Why be concerned about such nebulous things as *rights* when your immediate physical needs are being taken care of by the government?

However, to paraphrase Gerald Ford, a government that is big enough to give everyone everything is, of course, big enough to take everything away. In tyrannies throughout time, governments that have wielded great power have attempted to conform citizens, by force, to the ruler's, or ruling class's, way of thinking. As people have abdicated their rights in exchange for food, shelter, and care, the state then has the ability to take such things away, and to take them away, based on "wrong views" or moral codes or archaic beliefs in absolutes which inform an individual's life and decisions. This has been true from the time of the Roman Empire until today.

This is why the Founders firmly believed, and stated very clearly in the Declaration, "We hold these truths to be self-evident, that all men are created equal and that they are endowed by their Creator with certain unalienable rights, that among these are life, liberty and the pursuit of happiness." Rights given by a Creator exist outside of governments. Governments have nothing to do with an individual's natural rights, save one thing: to secure those rights, to protect them and take none of them away. Rights are not dependent upon governments but are inherent to all human beings.

They, like their Creator, are transcendent.

Yet governments that have grown too large naturally begin to encroach upon individual rights. It is the age-old tension between the individual and the state and those members of the state who desire to control everyone else. It is the question of where to draw the line between where state power ends and the individual's rights begin. So we as a people must ask ourselves what we believe about the role of government, the size and scope of government, and the purview of government. It is in asking those questions that we will find the answers to what we truly believe about individual rights.

CHAPTER TEN

To Secure the Blessings of Liberty: Building a Republic

———————— ◆ ————————

As he wrote down his observations of the American government, Alexis de Tocqueville admonished his readers: "To examine the Union before studying the state is to embark on a route strewn with obstacles. The form of the federal government of the United States appeared last; it was only a modification of the republic, a summary of the political principles spread through the entire society before it and subsisting independent of it."[120]

De Tocqueville recognized that the Constitution was an innovation in its own right but did not express completely innovative ideas. Instead, it articulated principles that had been at work in America ever since the first European settlers arrived. In succeeding years, as the population grew, Americans would learn to adapt such principles to their unique national circumstances.

For this reason, when the members of the Convention

---

120   de Tocqueville, 56.

presented the Constitution to the states for ratification, they knew that they would have to convince the people that the document did not so much propose a brand new political order as it provided a means of protecting the old one.

Federalism

"It has been frequently remarked," wrote Alexander Hamilton in the opening essay of *The Federalist Papers*, "that it seems to have been reserved to the people of this country, by their conduct and example, to decide the important question, whether societies of men are really capable or not of establishing good government from reflection or choice, or whether they are forever destined to depend, for their political constitutions, on accident and force."[121]

When the Convention adjourned on September 17, Hamilton promptly returned to New York to devise a strategy. He knew that New York would be one of the toughest battlegrounds for ratification. He summoned James Madison and New York native John Jay, and the three set to work writing dozens of essays, each one carefully explaining and defending a different aspect of the Constitution. The letters were published, at the rate of one a day, in various New York newspapers for public consumption.

The first issue addressed in *The Federalist Papers*, as these essays were called collectively, was the relationship between the national government and the state legislatures. Although it was

---

121   Alexander Hamilton, James Madison and John Jay, *The Federalist Papers*, ed. Garry Wills (New York: Bantam Books, 1982), 2.

clearly evident by this time that America could not survive as a confederacy, many Americans still insisted that a union of the states, headed by a national government, would threaten their freedoms. Was it possible for two "governments" to peacefully coexist?

James Madison tried to give the people a different perspective. "The Federal and State Governments are in fact but different agents and trustees of the people," he insisted, "instituted with different powers, and designated for different purposes. The adversaries of the Constitution seem to have lost sight of the people altogether in their reasoning on the subject; and to have viewed these different establishments . . . as mutual rivals and enemies."[122]

Hamilton, in turn, explained to the people that the safety and well-being of the states actually depended upon a strong national administration. "[T]he vigour of government is essential to the security of liberty," he said. If the states refuse to unite, "we shall be driven to the alternative, either of taking refuge at once in the arms of monarchy, or of splitting ourselves into an infinity of little jealous, clashing, tumultuous commonwealths, the wretched nurseries of unceasing discord and the miserable objects of universal pity or contempt."[123]

Hamilton specified three aspects of government that belonged, of necessity, under national authority. The first of these was the raising of revenue. After all, without funds, the government was helpless to perform its duties. Hamilton explained that the "most palpable defect of the subsisting confederation is the total want of

122   *Ibid.*, 237.
123   *Ibid.*, 4, 39.

a SANCTION to its laws." The first step toward rectifying this situation was enabling the government to raise revenue. Accordingly, the first power assigned to Congress, found in Article I, Section 8 of the Constitution, is the authority to "lay and collect taxes, duties, imposts [a duty on imported goods], and excises, to pay the debts and provide for the common defense and general welfare of the United States." The paragraph closes with the reminder that "all duties, imposts, and excises, shall be *uniform* throughout the United States."[124]

The second power that Hamilton recommended to the national government was the ability to regulate commerce. Under the Articles of Confederation, each of the 13 states had established its own rules regarding trade, with disastrous results. The "interfering and unneighbourly regulations of some States" encouraged hostility and dissension between them.[125] In addition, the states shared no common standards by which to conduct transactions with other countries. "No nation acquainted with the nature of our political association," stated Hamilton, "would be unwise enough to enter into stipulations with the United States . . . [upon being] apprised that the engagements on the part of the Union, might at any moment be violated by its members."[126]

Consequently, the Founders gave Congress the power to "regulate commerce with foreign nations, and among the several states, and with the Indian tribes," to establish a common currency

---

124   Emphasis added.
125   Federalist., 104.
126   *Ibid.*, 103.

and exchange rates, and to determine laws concerning bankruptcy and counterfeiting.[127]

The third major responsibility given to the national government was the power of defense. Americans feared that putting defense in the hands of the national government would subject them to the danger of standing armies. To prevent this capability, many argued that each state should be in charge of its own defense. Madison argued strongly against this, saying that a host of men with several different allegiances would expose the country to more danger than would a group of men under the national government. "Who [is] so likely to make suitable provisions for the public defense," he said, "as that body to which the guardianship of the public safety is confided—which, at the center of information, will best understand the extent and urgency of the dangers that threaten—as a representative of the WHOLE will feel itself most deeply interested in the preservation of every part?"[128] The Founders proceeded to give Congress the power to declare war, to establish and maintain both an army and a navy, and to "define and punish piracies and felonies committed on the high seas."

Despite the assurances that national power would be confined within these constitutional limits, many Americans still worried that the states would be overrun by the federal government. After all, the Convention had invested Congress with unprecedented power over taxes, over the economy, and over the military. Furthermore, the Constitution said nothing about the power

---

127   *U.S. Constitution*, Art. I, Sec. 8.
128   Federalist, 114.

supposedly retained by the states. In fact, the closest it came to even addressing state power was Article IV, Section 4, which read: "The United States shall guarantee to every state in this Union a republican form of government. . . ." The small states were outraged at what appeared to be a total eradication of state authority.

James Madison claimed that the opposite was true. "The powers delegated by the proposed Constitution to the Federal Government, are few and defined," he insisted. "Those which are to remain in the State Governments are numerous and indefinite."[129] In other words, the powers of the national government were *specified*, and thus could be held in check; the powers of the states were *implied* and open to wide interpretation; therefore, providing leverage against the national government.

Separation of Powers

"In the compound republic of America," wrote Madison, "the power surrendered by the people is first divided between two distinct governments, and then the portion allotted to each, subdivided among distinct and separate departments. Hence a double security arises to the rights of the people. The different governments will controul [original spelling retained] each other; at the same time that each will be controuled by itself."[130]

The Founding Fathers believed that the quickest path to tyranny was the concentration of power in a single entity or in the hands of a few. If there is one fundamental truth that the Founders

---

129   *Ibid.*, 236.
130   *Ibid.*, 264.

understood, it was that power should never be concentrated in the hands of imperfect human beings. In order to protect the American people from this danger, they determined to distribute power among as many different hands as possible; they believed in the diffusion of power and built that belief into almost every aspect of our constitutional republic. They were well enough acquainted with the nature of power to know that "a mere demarkation [original spelling retained] on parchment" would be unable to keep different powers in place. The only way to confine political power, said Madison, is "by so contriving the *interior* structure of the government, as that its several constituent parts may, by their mutual relations, be the means of keeping each other in their proper places."[131]

Historically, most societies had been built on a hierarchical pattern, descending in order from the *one* to the *few* to the *many*. These categories were usually filled, respectively, by a king, an aristocracy, and the common people. Theoretically, the tension between these classes helped to keep them in balance with each other.

America, however, represented a new societal pattern. She had been built, so to speak, from the bottom up. Her people had never needed a king to rule them; instead, they and their representatives *ruled themselves*, looking to their Creator and to the law as their ultimate authorities. America had no class system or class interest. Instead, all Americans were united by the same primary interest, that of protecting their freedom. Therefore, the Founders separated the powers of the American government according to their

---

131   *Ibid.*, 261. Emphasis added.

responsibilities, producing three branches: the **Legislative branch** was given the power to make law, the **Executive branch**, the power to enforce law, and the **Judicial branch**, the charge of interpreting the Constitutionality of the law.[132]

This practice of separating powers was not new. Britain, for example, had divided political power between the king and Parliament, and then divided Parliament into the Houses of Lords and Commons. The Founders admired this example but wanted to improve upon it. Believing the people to be the "only legitimate fountain of power," the Founders sought to construct the government in such a way that it would ultimately answer back to the people. The first means of doing this was ensuring that the different branches keep each other in check. "[T]he great security against a gradual concentration of the several powers in the same department," said Madison, "consists in giving to those who administer each department the necessary constitutional means, and personal motives, to resist encroachments of the others."[133]

Controlling the Effects of Faction

As they deliberated over the structure of the new government, the delegates in Philadelphia frequently consulted the political examples of past civilizations, both the good and the bad. Because of their classical training, the Founders were well acquainted with the history and government of ancient Athens. In the fifth century before Christ, the Greek ruler Pericles (c. 495-429 B.C.)

---

132   Garry Wills, introduction to Federalist, xvi-xvii.
133   Federalist, 262.

had established a form of government in Athens which allowed the participation of all free citizens. During the late 1700s, European scholars praised this "Golden Age" of Athens, claiming that it had introduced the idea of democracy to the world. However, while the Founders appreciated the philosophical and artistic legacy of the Greeks, they had a rather low opinion of their politics.

They knew that the Greeks, while instituting popular sovereignty, had neglected to impose proper restraints on the people's exercise of power. Citizens began using their "liberty" as an excuse to indulge their pride and avarice; they bribed one another, cheated one another, and took one another to court, using the law as a political weapon to settle political and personal differences. As the people became focused solely on satisfying their own desires, they fell prey to demagogues and swindlers who promised to meet their needs. The government was soon plagued by factions. Finally, unable to sustain order or to defend the country from invasion, Greece became a victim of foreign conquest. The Golden Age of Greece lasted less than 75 years.[134]

"What bitter anguish would not the people of Athens have often escaped, if their government had contained . . . a safeguard against the tyranny of their own passions?" wrote Madison of this sobering tale. How could they, the Founding Fathers, afford Americans freedom and yet prevent them from abusing it? How could the people maintain their sovereignty without degenerating into hostile factions?

---

134   Kirk, 69-71.

Madison thought long and hard on this subject. "By a faction," he wrote, "I understand a number of citizens . . . who are united and actuated by some common impulse of passion, or of interest, adverse to the rights of other citizens, or to the permanent and aggregate interests of the community.[135] There are only two possible ways, he said, to mitigate the danger of faction. One, he wrote, is to prevent faction altogether. This could only be achieved by depriving citizens the freedom of association or by forcing all citizens to have the same opinion on all subjects. Neither of these, of course, is satisfactory (or practical), wrote Madison, as each would destroy the whole purpose of preventing faction, which is to preserve liberty. "Liberty is to faction, what air is to fire, an ailment without which it instantly expires," he wrote.[136]

Faction, in a sense, is a by-product of liberty, and the only way to prevent faction altogether is to prevent liberty—an unacceptable solution. It is just as unacceptable, not to mention impossible, to force all citizens to have the same opinion on all subjects. "The inference to which we are [then] brought," he concluded, "is, that the *causes* of faction cannot be removed; and that relief is only to be sought in the means of controlling its *effects*."[137]

The power of a faction resides in the ability of its members to communicate with each other—"to concert and carry into effect schemes of oppression." But if the members of a faction are prevented from collaborating on a regular basis, will not that

---

135   *The Federalist*, 43.
136   *Ibid.*
137   *Ibid.*, 45.

faction cease to operate effectively? If a people are scattered over a wide area, they will be unable to form factions. Now, in a relatively small society, this solution would prove unworkable because every citizen would be within easy access of one another. But in America, with its extensive territory and huge population—scattered across 13 different states and a wilderness—forming a faction was not so simple. Even a sinister genius would be at pains to mobilize followers over such a large area.[138] "The influence of factious leaders may kindle a flame within their particular States, but will be unable to spread a general conflagration through the other States," wrote Madison.[139] "In the extent and proper structure of the Union, therefore, we behold a Republican remedy for the diseases most incident to Republican Government."[140]

As the people slowly began to realize the wisdom of the Founders' arguments, they still feared the novelty of the constitutional scheme. Even if the Constitution *did* reaffirm the old order, its proposed model of government had never been tried before. Was it wise then, for an entire nation to embark on an untrodden path? Some said no. But Madison urged the people to remember that America was a land of novelties, and that they need not be afraid of another:

> Is it not the glory of the people of America, that
> whilst they have paid a decent regard to the opinions of

---

138   *Ibid.*, 46.
139   *Ibid.*, 48.
140   *Ibid.*, 49.

former times and other nations, they have not suffered a blind veneration for antiquity, for custom, or for names, to overrule the suggestions of their own good sense, the knowledge of their own situation, and the lessons of their own experience? To this manly spirit, posterity will be indebted for the possession, and the world for the example of the numerous innovations displayed on the American theatre, in favor of private rights and public happiness.[141]

Britain had tried to impose unconstitutional "novelties" upon the colonies, and Americans had succeeded in defending their rights. They knew that they needed to boldly face the challenges ahead, pressing on to greater glory as a free and unified nation.

---

141   *Ibid.*, 66-67.

CHAPTER ELEVEN
An Essential Part of Every Healthy Republic: Private Property

◆

Among all the rights the Founders believed inherent to human beings, and that were to be safeguarded by the government, was the right to private property. In fact, one could argue that it was considered among one of the greatest rights by the Founders. It was the essence of freedom for an individual to consider his faculties, his land, his property, to be his very own. For John Locke, the British philosopher who broke onto the European philosophical scene with his *Second Treatise of Government* in the late 17th century and who heavily influenced the Founders' thinking, the "first object of government created by the consent of the governed is to protect the right to property."[142]

But for Locke and the Founders, property was not just simply physical things: land or houses or any goods an individual might own. It is much more than that: property is our faculties, our

---

142   Patrick, 30.

ideas, our freedom and liberty. All of these things that are unique to an individual are the private property of the individual. The destruction of the idea of true private ownership has been the aim of socialists for centuries, from the ideas of state-run production, to Progressives who view private property, and the capitalist system that relies upon property ownership, as evil. But it is the idea of private property, and rights and responsibilities, ideas that are implicit in the 8th Commandment ("Thou shalt not steal"), that gives rise to the ideals of stewardship and respecting the rights and property of others.

While many Americans know that the Pilgrims were a small band of English Protestant Separatists who sailed to America on the *Mayflower*, landing in Massachusetts 1620. What many don't know is that the Pilgrims, while setting up their new community, gave communism a try. The experiment was born out of necessity. The Pilgrims were ill-prepared for life in the New World. During their first winter in America, half of them died from disease. As their supplies ran low, the surviving Pilgrims knew they would need to cultivate crops so they wouldn't starve to death. The leaders decided it would be best for everyone in the community to equally share both labor and provisions. No one would own private land. All property would be maintained by the community as a whole. The men would work in communal fields. The women would tend to communal chores. Food and clothing would be distributed to families in proportion to their number. The leaders hoped this communal approach would bring the population together and set them on the path to prosperity.

The experiment was an unmitigated disaster.

Despite their combined efforts, the workers couldn't seem to produce a good crop. Neighbors began to bicker with each other. The men resented working to feed other families when their own families were hungry. The diligent workers resented taking home only as much food as the weak or lazy. The women resented cooking other men's meals and washing other men's clothes—it made them feel like slaves, they said. People began to "call in sick" and make excuses not to work at all.[143]

The leaders revisited their plan. The Pilgrims couldn't afford to be philosophical about their situation. They were a world away from everything they knew. Their group was inexperienced, small in number and huddled on the edge of an untamed wilderness. They had one shot at survival. And in this case, death wouldn't discriminate—rich and poor would die together.

So they scrapped the commune model and instead entrusted a portion of land to each family. The improvement was immediate. William Bradford, a Pilgrim leader who kept a detailed history of the community's early years, marveled at the result. "This had very good success," he wrote, "for it made all hands very industrious, so as much more corn was planted than otherwise would have been by any means the Governor or any other could use . . . and gave far better content."[144]

---

143   William Bradford, *Of Plymouth Plantation*, 1620–1647. Edited by Samuel Eliot Morison. New York: Modern Library, 1967. Excerpt accessed at The Founders' Constitution, http://press-pubs.uchicago.edu/founders/documents/v1ch16s1.html/.
144   *Ibid.*

Besides eventually getting a bumper crop, the settlers began to respect each other again. They all took more responsibility for their own work and had a greater appreciation for the work of others. As individual families thrived, the community as a whole thrived.

Needless to say, that was the end of communism for the Pilgrims. If roughly 100 starving people—dependent on each other for survival, and good Christians at that—couldn't successfully "hold all things in common," who could? The Pilgrims had stumbled upon a principle that would be staunchly defended 150 years later by their descendants: Not only is private property a foundational tenet of a free and prosperous society, it is a realistic way of dealing with human nature—directing it in a way that benefits the whole community.

In Search of Utopia

In a way, the Pilgrims couldn't be blamed for thinking the communist or communal model might work. The idea of abolishing private property for the supposed benefit of the community has been around for centuries. Private property has occupied the writings of some of history's greatest thinkers and has been at the crux of the most notorious social revolutions. In Western Civilization in particular, private property has at times been extolled as civil society's greatest good and condemned as its greatest evil. And in the 18th century, this debate came straight to America's doorstep, where the right to private property took on a unique meaning.

The history-long discussion over private property has nearly always hinged on the question of how to create an orderly and peaceful society. Philosophers, politicians, and religious leaders have all struggled to define the best society—that state of perfection where humans live happily and peacefully with one another. Such thinkers have generally fallen into one of two categories: those who believe humans are capable of bettering themselves and bringing order to society through their own efforts, and those who believe humans are essentially *incapable* of ordering their lives without the influence of transcendent principles. The former have tended to treat private property as a man-made convention, a potential source of evil that needs to be heavily regulated or removed altogether. The latter have treated it as a natural right and a pillar of freedom that must be guarded with the utmost care. Traditionally, Americans have taken the latter view.

While it is impossible to absolutely pinpoint the origins of debate over private property, we know the discussion began early in history; considering the implicit understanding of the 8th Commandment, historians estimate that Moses and the Ten Commandments occurred around the mid-14th century B.C. so this is a debate that has occurred for over 3,000 years. One of the earliest well-known figures to challenge private property was the Greek philosopher Plato (died c. 347 B.C.). Living in Athens during a period of cultural decline, Plato was distressed to see wars raging abroad and depravity increasing at home.[145] Through his philosophical discourses, he sought the "key" to order and virtue in human society. In *The Republic*, Plato—through the character of

---

145   Kirk, 85.

his former teacher, Socrates—pondered what this virtuous society would look like. If people were to live in harmony with each other, he reasoned, they would need to abandon social conventions that prompted strife. Whatever encouraged greed, envy, dishonesty, and selfishness would need to go. "[W]here there is no common but only private feeling a State is disorganized," wrote Plato in *The Republic*. "Such differences commonly originate in a disagreement about the use of the terms 'mine' and 'not mine,' 'his' and 'not his.'"[146]

Private property—the chief tool for distinguishing between "mine" and "not mine"—was a primary culprit of this disunity in Plato's thinking. Thus, in this ideal society, the most prominent citizens, such as "guardians" of the state, would be forbidden to hold private property. They would not be permitted to own houses, land, or material possessions, but would share all such things with the community. This would free them from worldly distractions and petty quarrels, allowing them to "preserve their true character" and virtue as guardians of the state.[147]

On the surface, this plan made sense. If a society was to have peace, it needed to remove the supposed causes of strife—in this case, material objects such as private property. Interestingly enough, however, Plato and his fellow philosophers intuitively recognized two other conditions that would be required for this model to work, even in theory. First, if the guardians couldn't hold any private

---

146   Plato, *The Republic*, Book V., accessed at Project Gutenberg, http://www.gutenberg.org/files/1497/1497-h/1497-h.htm#link2H_4_0008 (The Project Gutenberg EBook of The Republic, by Plato).
147   *Ibid.*

possessions, someone else would still have to provide for them. (In *The Republic*, this obligation apparently falls to other citizens, who would pay the guardians with food.) Second, if the guardians were to be *truly* free from all private cares and influences, they would have to share not only all material possessions with their neighbors, but their wives and children as well. After all, a man with a wife and children puts his family's needs above the needs of the community. He provides a home only for them and expends his labor especially on their behalf. In a communist context then, a family becomes a harmful influence, drawing a person's affections away from the community and toward "*private* pleasures and pains."[148] In Plato's *Republic*, a man should not be able to call one woman *his* wife; she should be a wife to many. And he should not call any one child *his* child; all children should be raised collectively by the community so that no citizen can distinguish or favor his child above another's.

   This discourse, though focused only on an imaginary society, touched on the "problem" of tampering with private property: If "mine" and "not mine" are harmful distinctions for a community, then how far is that community able to go in eradicating such differences? After all, if a society has no problem taking away a person's house, why would it have a problem taking away anything else that belongs to an individual, as long as it benefits the community? Who decides what *truly* belongs to the individual as a right?

---

148   *Ibid.* Emphasis added.

A Natural Right

Centuries after Plato, a different approach to private property was at work in medieval Europe. This approach taught that property was a *natural right* given by God to human beings for their benefit. As such, an individual's private property was sacred; it couldn't be violated, and it couldn't be seized by a temporal authority without due process of law. This concept, while ancient in origin, gained particular expression in England. The English encapsulated this idea in many of their landmark documents throughout history, including the Magna Carta (1215) and the English Bill of Rights (1689). But the right of private property had been preserved even long before this in *unwritten* form, in England's ancient common law. Through the common law, rich and poor alike understood that it was wrong for one person to unjustly take the property of another. As Blackstone later articulated in his 18th-century *Commentaries on the Laws of England*: "[B]y a variety of antient statutes it is enacted, that no man's lands or goods shall be seised [original spelling retained] into the king's hands, against the great charter, and the law of the land; and that no man shall be disinherited, nor put out of his franchises or freehold, unless he be duly brought to answer, and be forejudged by course of law; and if anything be done to the contrary, it shall be redressed, and holden for none."[149]

While this viewpoint clarified property rights in regard to the

---

149   William Blackstone, *Commentaries on the Laws of England*, Volume 1. Accessed at The Founders' Constitution, http://press-pubs.uchicago.edu/founders/documents/v1ch16s5.html.

individual, how was this arrangement supposed to look in a society? How did a single person's right to maintain his property actually benefit the broader community? And what was government's role in regard to private property? As the Middle Ages gave way to the Modern Era and, then, to the Age of Enlightenment, these questions received more and more attention.

The Community Pitted Against the Individual

The late 17th and early 18th centuries ushered in the Age of Enlightenment. As scientific inquiry increased and ideas were more easily transmitted from place to place, people began to challenge the authority of old political and religious establishments. Social revolutions gained traction as the middle and lower classes began to chip away at the monarchical foundations of Europe. As concepts such as popular sovereignty grew in popularity, people began to debate what a truly modern government and society should look like—and where property ought to fit in the grand scheme.

With his *Second Treatise of Government* in 1690, Locke's purpose was to refute some of the prevailing political theories of his day. One of these was the "Divine Right of Kings," the doctrine that monarchs had absolute power given to them by God. The kings of Europe had used this doctrine for centuries to justify their power (including violent and arbitrary uses of it) over their subjects. Locke argued that this concept of government fell outside the created order. Government was, in fact, a man-made institution, developed for the safety and benefit of its citizens. Locke explained this by exploring society's origins. He wrote that man's "state of nature"—his original living condition before the evolution of towns, cities, and governments—was one of unbridled freedom and independence. God had created man a free being and had given him inherent rights to "life, liberty, and estate" (*estate* being another word for "property").[150] In this condition, a man could freely stake a claim in the wilderness, cultivate the land and fully enjoy its fruits. However, this primitive bliss also had its dangers. The individual had no sufficient means to defend himself or his property from other people, should the need arise.

People solved this problem, said Locke, by coming together and forming a civil society through voluntary association. The society provided the individual with the protection of laws and the security of a community. There was a trade-off, of course: People who chose to join the society had to surrender their personal sovereignty to the sovereignty of the new community. The individual agreed to live under the laws and government of the society, and the government agreed to protect him and his property. Locke thus concluded that the "great and *chief end* therefore, of Mens uniting into Commonwealths, and putting themselves under Government, *is the Preservation of their Property.*"[151]

Locke's ideas, of which the previous is only a small part,

---

150   John Locke, *Second Treatise of Government*, Section 87, accessed at http://www.justiceharvard.org/resources/john-locke-second-treatise-of-government-1690/.

151   John Locke, excerpted from *Second Treatise*, Chapter IX, accessed at The Founders' Constitution site of the University of Chicago, http://press-pubs.uchicago.edu/founders/documents/v1ch16s3.html. Emphasis original.

would influence different contemporary movements but in different ways. The American Founding Fathers adhered to parts of Locke's writings, particularly to the idea that a government's purpose was to protect the property of its citizens. But when it came to the idea of the individual surrendering his sovereignty to the sovereignty of the community, Locke perhaps gave the community too much credit. How could an amorphous human society be trusted to do what was right for the individual? What if a society decided it knew better than the individual what was right *for* the individual?

Such dilemmas came into focus later in France. Enlightenment thinker Jean-Jacques Rousseau (1712–1778), writing several years before the French Revolution, went much further than Locke in his confidence of the community.[152] Rousseau suggested that the proper way for a society to govern itself was through the "general will" of the people. The general will is sovereign, for "the general will alone can direct the State according to the object for which it was instituted, i.e., the common good."[153] The general will is qualified to decide the common good, explained Rousseau, because it "considers only the common interest," while an individual citizen "takes private interest into account."[154]

This sounds nice in theory, but what if the general will decides that private property—or any other individual rights—are *not* in the common good? If we are to judge by some of Rousseau's

---

152   Kirk, 286-287.
153   Jean-Jacques Rousseau, *Social Contract: Book II*, accessed at The Constitution Society, http://www.constitution.org/jjr/socon_02.htm.
154   *Ibid.*

other writings, private property rights don't stand much of a chance in his model. To Rousseau, property was a source of social inequality and all the evils that flowed from it. It was purely a man-made convention, a corrupting influence that soiled man's primitive and innocent nature:

> The first man, who, after enclosing a piece of ground, took it into his head to say, "This is mine," and found people simple enough to believe him, was the true founder of civil society. How many crimes, how many wars, how many murders, how many misfortunes and horrors, would that man have saved the human species, who pulling up the stakes or filling up the ditches should have cried to his fellows: Be sure not to listen to this imposter; you are lost, if you forget that the fruits of the earth belong equally to us all, and the earth itself to nobody![155]

After all is said and done, is there any way to have a society that both respects the individual's private property rights, but also *benefits* from those rights?

A Right to Property, and a Property in Rights

The American Founding Fathers studied many of history's

---

155   Jean-Jacques Rousseau, *A Discourse Upon The Origin And The Foundation Of The Inequality Among Mankind*, accessed at Project Gutenberg, http://www.gutenberg.org/cache/epub/11136/pg11136.html (The Project Gutenberg EBook of A Discourse Upon The Origin And The Foundation Of The Inequality Among Mankind, by Jean-Jacques Rousseau).

greatest philosophers and political theorists. They kept up with the times and understood the significance of the era in which they lived. They too, like so many of the philosophers, saw the need for order and harmony in human society. But unlike many others, they believed the right to own property was *key* to such order and prosperity, rather than a hindrance to it.

The Founders may have been classicists in their training, but they were also Judeo-Christian in thought, English in heritage and practical in temperament. These influences made a significant difference in their approach to private property. As Judeo-Christians, the Founders believed that human beings were created in the image of God and were highly capable of creating a sophisticated, prosperous, and free society. But they also believed that humans were inherently corrupt and could build such a society only upon transcendent—not solely man-made—principles. This is why they hallowed the concept of natural rights: God had bestowed these rights, and therefore only God could revoke them. No temporal power had a right to violate or deny these rights.

As Englishmen in heritage, the Founders were heavily influenced by England's traditional approach to property through the concept of natural rights and the common law. No one could touch another's property rights without due process of law. And everyone—king and commoner alike—were bound *equally* by the law and stood equal before it.

Being practical in temperament, the Founders looked for what *worked* in experience as they created America's government and system of laws. Even in pre-Revolutionary America, private property was the *rule*, not just a theory. At the beginning of European migration, the New World had offered countless acres of wild land to anyone who was willing to work hard and carve out a life in the wilderness. For early American settlers, private property had not only offered the sole means of survival, but had also laid the foundation for flourishing farms, families, communities, and, eventually, colonies. In this way, America had the unique opportunity of forming a distinct culture and complete way of life before it even became a nation, and this culture was based largely on private property. So from the beginning, private property was not simply a "nice to have"—it was the *rule*, and it was the foundation of Americans' independence and freedom. So when the Founders began designing a new government, they looked for what accommodated the freedoms and rights already in operation on American soil.

But the Founders went a step further. A person's property was sacred because it intertwined with his very personhood. To the Founders, "property" meant much more than land, houses, money and material possessions. The full definition of property, wrote James Madison, "embraces every thing to which a man may attach a value and have a right; and *which leaves to every one else the like advantage.*"[156] Thus, property includes: A person's opinion and his right to communicate it freely, a person's religious beliefs and his freedom to profess and practice those beliefs (conscience being "the

---

156   James Madison, *Property*, dated March 29, 1792. Excerpted from *The Papers of James Madison at The Founders' Constitution*, accessed at http://press-pubs.uchi-cago.edu/founders/documents/v1ch16s23.html. Emphasis original.

most sacred of all property"), personal safety, and liberty, which, Madison notes, includes freedom from "arbitrary seizures of one class of citizens for the service of the rest." Property also includes a person's free use of his faculties (skills, talents and abilities), choice of occupation, and the ability to earn and keep wealth. For, as Madison explains, "a just security to property is not afforded by that government, under which unequal taxes oppress one species of property and reward another species, where arbitrary taxes invade the domestic sanctuaries of the rich, and excessive taxes grind the faces of the poor."

"In a word," said Madison, "as man is said to have a right to his property, he may be equally said to have a property in his rights." This is precisely why the Founders took property violations so seriously. A violation of one's property is an assault on all his other rights. When the government is allowed to encroach on one individual right, it will inevitably encroach on all the others. Such a government is not just and such a people are not free.

And while the Founders cared about individual rights, they also believed the right to property benefited the community in many of the same ways sought by the utopists. First, allowing people the right to property harnesses the power of self-interest. Private property engages a person's energy and motivates him to work for himself and his family. He knows he will rise or fall based on his own efforts. However, self-interest alone is not enough to produce a free, happy society. It must be balanced and directed in ways that are beneficial to the whole community.

When human beings are held *responsible* for their own property, there exists an intangible restraint, holding the individual accountable for his conduct and giving him a healthy way to relate to the community. The citizen who is responsible for his own property has an incentive to think ahead and to be productive. He naturally wants what is good for his community because it will also be good for him. Ideally, property also produces in the citizen an empathy for his neighbors, who are also being held responsible for their labor and possessions. When people cease to be held responsible—for their property, their labor, their families, or anything else that can truly be called their "own"—freedom loses its meaning. When nothing is expected of the individual and all his needs are simply provided to him as an entitlement, his heart begins to grow cold and turn inward.

While it is true that the Founders thought mostly about property in regards to male ownership, many women since the founding have been property owners. Nevertheless, it was mostly males who owned properties and dominated that aspect of life during this era. As American notions of liberty expanded over the decades, property in America came to be understood as the longing, by right, of any individual, male or female, and for people of all ethnic or national backgrounds.

The Threat Today

In America, private property is integral to who we are. A government cutting away at that right undermines the very idea that people have an inviolable right to call something their own.

Unfortunately, in America, we are increasingly influenced by the idea that private property is simply an old social convention—something that can be manipulated or pushed aside at any time for the "benefit" of the community. A classic example is the notorious 2005 case *Kelo v. City of New London*. In this instance, the town of New London, Connecticut, seized the private property of several citizens to sell to private developers. They justified this by saying that the developers would create jobs, increase tax revenues, and produce other benefits for the wider community. The Supreme Court, siding with New London against the private property owners, argued that this type of property seizure did not violate the Constitution.[157] The underlying message from the case? It's acceptable for the government to arbitrarily seize an individual's private property as long as it can make an argument that the seizure benefits the community. Suddenly, the individual's rights don't matter anymore and the government's word does.

However, a government doesn't have to physically take away someone's property to infringe on property rights. A government can implement arbitrary or unjust taxes, policies and legal hindrances that make it difficult for citizens to acquire or maintain their property. Any and all such infringements on property rights infringe not only on our property, but also on our freedom. To undermine private property rights is to undermine one of the essential foundations of our republic. As John Adams wrote in 1787,

---

157   "*KELO v. CITY OF NEW LONDON*," The Oyez Project at IIT Chicago-Kent College of Law, accessed May 8, 2013, http://www.oyez.org/cases/2000-2009/2004/2004_04_108.

"The moment the idea is admitted into society, that property is not as sacred as the laws of God, and that there is not a force of law and public justice to protect it, anarchy and tyranny commence. If 'Thou shalt not covet,' and 'Thou shalt not steal,' were not commandments of Heaven, they must be made inviolable precepts in every society, before it can be civilized or made free."[158]

---

158   John Adams, *A Defence of the Constitutions of Government of the United States*, 1787, accessed at http://press-pubs.uchicago.edu/founders/documents/v1ch16s15.html.

CHAPTER TWELVE
Constructing the Machinery of a Republic

———————◆———————

"In framing a government which is to be administered by men over men, the great difficulty lies in this: You must first enable the government to controul the governed; and in the next place, oblige it to controul itself [original spelling retained]."[159]

The Founding Fathers knew too well the human person's tendency to be corrupted by power. They believed that, without exception, any individual or group vested with unchecked authority would eventually abuse it. However, the men who drafted the Constitution also realized that power itself was not depraved—only its misuse. Law and liberty were not incompatible; in fact, the exercise of true freedom required strong, just, and enforced law.[160] Thus, in designing a government, the Founders' greatest challenge lay in striking a balance between law and liberty. How could they devise a government that would be strong enough to maintain order but

---

159 Madison, *Federalist 51*, The Federalist Papers, 262.
160 Kirk, 353.

would never encroach upon the rights, freedoms, and property of the people?

The mechanics of the American system reflect, in part, the era in which the Founders lived. Though their decisions in the Convention were influenced at a fundamental level by their peculiar understanding of order and of human nature, they derived the practical design for American government largely from contemporary political theory. The Founders developed their opinions in an age stimulated by scientific discovery. In the decades preceding the American Revolution, both Europe and America had been eagerly watching the progress of various scientists, ranging from Isaac Newton to the Convention's own Benjamin Franklin. Such men had begun to articulate the "laws of nature" and to define certain principles governing the universe. For Americans, these discoveries accorded with their belief that God had instilled an order in creation that permeated every aspect of life. This order, they believed, extended to human government.

In establishing the American government, the Founders were also heavily influenced by the French theorist Charles-Louis de Secondat, Baron de Montesquieu, whom many of them had studied as schoolboys. Montesquieu advocated what came to be known as the "separation of powers." Traditionally, in Western nations, governmental power was embodied in a single entity, such as an individual or a ruling body. Consequently, those who made law also had authority to interpret and enforce it. In most of these cases, the words and wishes of the ruling authority gradually *became* the law.

Montesquieu decried this abuse of power. If human beings were to create a society in which no individual was above the law, they needed to devise a system that impacted its rulers in the same manner as its subjects. Why not, suggested Montesquieu, divide and allocate the power of the government in such a way that no one entity can dominate more than any other? Separate the legislative, executive and judicial powers from one another, and the tension between them will keep each in its proper place.

This is the beauty of our Constitution: The Founders believed that individual rights should be enumerated; thus our Bill of Rights. Yet they also believed that those stated rights on paper were mere "parchment barriers" against tyranny and abuse of power. It was the mechanisms and construction of our republic, with its separation of powers and its diffusion of power that were the real barriers against tyranny, for those concepts in action prevent concentrated power.

Montesquieu's practical theory resounded with the American people. It coincided with their belief that the purpose of government was not to protect the authority of rulers from the people, but to protect the sovereignty of the people from their rulers. Thus, the main goal of the members at the Constitutional Convention was to establish a government in which the three branches of government not only maintained their proper places, but also worked together in such a way as to create the "bounds of ordered liberty," within which an imperfect humanity could experience as much freedom as is possible in an imperfect world.

The Legislative Branch

The first branch to which the Founders turned their creative attention was the legislative, the most complex of the three. The Founders' first undertaking was to divide the legislative branch into two bodies; the House of Representatives and the Senate. The House was to be a representative body, consisting of a certain number of officials from each state, depending on population. Representatives were elected by popular vote for two-year terms. The Senate, while also a representative body, was to operate less as a voice for the people and more as a diplomatic body, guarding the interests of the state governments. Each state legislature was to elect two senators to serve a term of six years in Congress. All legislative activity would require the input and approval of both of these bodies, forcing them to work together for the good of the nation.

As the two houses of Congress check each other, they are both checked from the outside by the Executive branch. When the House and Senate pass a bill, it must be sent to the executive, or President, for his approval. If he refuses to sign it, the bill must go back to Congress for reconsideration. However, both the executive branch and Congress are kept in check indirectly by the judicial branch, headed by the Supreme Court. The Court has constitutional power to judge cases involving ambassadors and other public ministers, or disputes to which a state or citizens from different states are party. Supreme Court justices are the only officials in the federal government who hold their offices for life—another advantage against the other two branches.

A frequent complaint against the American government is that its design is too complicated, and that its many checks and balances make legislation unnecessarily difficult. However, this is exactly what the Founders intended. They believed that if the federal process was sufficiently complex, only the worthiest and most beneficial legislation would become law. In addition, they believed that unavoidable delays would force legislators to consider and reconsider the merits of a bill. "[I]t is the reason of the public alone that ought to controul and regulate the government," wrote Madison. "The passions ought to be controuled and regulated by the government."[161]

The Founders recognized that the power to make laws was superior to all others a government might possess. For this reason, they designed the legislature as a *representative* body to ensure that the task of governing would rest, ultimately, in the hands of the people. In our republic, power flows from the people. Accordingly, in theory, Congress is to exercise some of the most significant power in the land. The first article of the Constitution specifies that Congress alone has power to collect taxes, regulate commerce, declare war, maintain the armed forces, confirm Presidential nominees, and to establish currency, thereby addressing many of the weaknesses of the Articles of Confederation. In addition, Congress is responsible for establishing post offices, granting patents, and instituting rules of naturalization.

However, the Founders worried that instilling too much

---

161   *Ibid.*, 258.

authority in a single assembly would lead to legislative tyranny. They were concerned also that a body representing the people according to population only would decrease the influence of state governments and centralize power to a dangerous extent. The challenge of striking a balance between the power of the people and the power of the states, as has been previously pointed out, generated the greatest controversy of the Constitutional Convention.

The Founders' intent in dividing Congress into two houses was to create a productive tension between them, resulting in just and equitable legislation. They believed that if the legislative process was sufficiently complex, only the most necessary and deliberate proposals would emerge as law. Each house was built upon a different mode of representation, and each now operates under a distinct set of rules, yet no law can be passed without the approval of both.

Designing a House of Representatives was among the first orders of business at the Constitutional Convention. The Founders believed that the House, as the national repository for public opinion, should communicate with the people as directly as possible. "As it is essential to liberty that the government in general, should have a common interest with the people," wrote James Madison, "so it is particularly essential that the [House] should have an immediate dependence on, and an intimate sympathy with the people."[162] Accordingly, representatives are elected by popular vote in each state, the number of officials being determined by state population. The Founders placed few restrictions on eligibility for

---

162   Madison, *Federalist 52*, The Federalist Papers, 267.

office, believing that the representatives of the people ought to reflect them appropriately. The only requirements for office were that a candidate be at least 25 years old, that he be no less than seven years a resident of the United States, that he dwell in the state he planned to represent, and that he hold no other office at the time of his candidacy.

While the statute regarding eligibility was passed with little debate, a matter of more controversy among the Founders was that of the duration of service. Americans, accustomed to keeping a close eye on their public officials, had traditionally favored one-year terms for state legislators. Some states, such as Connecticut and Rhode Island, allowed representatives to serve no more than six months at a time.[163] While most agreed that elections should be held regularly, some feared that frequent turnover would make the country vulnerable. Madison argued that a year was an insufficient length of time for representatives to build experience. "No one," he said, "can be a competent legislator who does not add to an upright intention and a sound judgment, a certain degree of knowledge of the subjects on which he is to legislate."[164] Instead, he successfully proposed a term of two years, believing it both short enough to keep representatives dependent upon the people's good opinion, and long enough for the representatives to improve their skills.

To bolster its power, the Founders were certain to assign to the House alone a significant privilege. Modeled in many respects after the British House of Commons, the House retains "power of

---

163   Ibid., *Federalist Nos. 52-53*; 268, 271.
164   Ibid., *Federalist 53*, 272.

the purse," or the ability to originate legislation for raising taxes. This prerogative is the assembly's most compelling advantage against the other branches of government.

At the same time that they championed the rights of the people, the Founding Fathers recognized the public's tendency toward rash and thoughtless action. "[T]here are particular moments in public affairs," wrote James Madison, "when the people, stimulated by some irregular passion . . . may call for measures which they themselves will afterwards be the most ready to lament and condemn." In certain societies, the remedy for such a crisis is to transfer authority from the people to a dictator or a powerful group of statesmen. But in America's free society, this is not an option. "In these critical moments," proposed Madison, "how salutary will be the interference of some temperate and respectable body of citizens . . . to suspend the blow mediated by the people against themselves, until reason, justice and truth, can regain their authority over the public mind?"[165]

The Founders provided for this esteemed "body of citizens" in the form of the Senate. The Senate, representing the interests of the states, would lend a deliberative and diplomatic tenor to the legislative process and supply expertise that might be lacking in the House. "[G]ood government implies two things," wrote Madison. "[F]irst, fidelity to the object of government, which is the happiness of the people; secondly, a knowledge of the means by which that object can be best attained." Madison commented that while many

---

165   *Ibid., Federalist 63*, 320.

political structures possess neither of these qualities, the American system tended to fall short, particularly on the latter. Americans, he implied, are patriotic and well-meaning but often lack skill and knowledge to accomplish their legislative goals. [166]

The Senate was an answer to this dilemma. The Founders, intending for the Senate to be the more astute body of Congress, empowered it to consult on foreign affairs. Article II of the Constitution authorizes the assembly to approve the actions of the Executive Branch in the drafting of treaties and in the appointment of ambassadors, consuls, and justices.

The Senate's distinctive character caused it to differ from the House in many ways, the first and most significant difference being its mode of representation. While the House represents the population proportionately, and is called the People's House, the Senate was truly intended to serve the interests of the states through equal representation; for all intents and purposes it was meant to be the *States'* House. As de Tocqueville wrote, "The principle of the independence of the states triumphed in the formation of the Senate; the dogma of national sovereignty, in the composition of the House of Representatives."[167] Consisting of only two members from each state, the Senate is naturally much smaller than the House. But its size and design guaranteed that states had rights and a powerful voice in the new federal government and that every state would have an equal voice in debate, making the environment conducive to calm discussion.

The Founders created a second distinction between the

---

166   *Ibid., Federalist 62*, 316.
167   de Tocqueville, 111.

House and Senate by placing senatorial elections in the hands of the state assemblies. The Founders believed that this power was appropriate to state legislators, not only because the latter were acquainted with the interests of their respective states, but also because their own political experience qualified them to select worthy candidates.

For the first 126 years of the republic, state legislators chose their various U.S. Senators, who served at the will and pleasure of the state's representatives. This changed in the early 20th century, when Robert La Follette, the Republican Progressive from Wisconsin, agitated for and achieved the direct election of Senators with the passage of the 17th Amendment. This action broke the balance of power between the chambers of Congress and unmoored Senators from their foremost priority of being representatives of states' interests. In the immediate, La Follette's concerns were understandable: The corruption of state party bosses by railroad corporations influenced those party bosses to induce the state legislators to select Senators who represented the corporations' interests, thereby corrupting the process. But the "reform" made Senators less accountable to their states and removed from the machinery of the republic the idea of the independence of the states by forcing them to surrender one of the most powerful voices they had in the nation's capital. In so doing, it helped pave the way for greater concentration of power in Washington, DC. In solving one ill, the "reform" of the 17th Amendment led to an even greater one and put in place one of the most pernicious poison pills in our republic, greatly undermining the idea of federalism and the 10th Amendment (which expresses the principle of Federalism and states' rights).

Thirdly, the Senate differs from the House in the requirements it places on candidates for office. To run for a Senate seat, an individual must be at least 30 years old instead of the House's 25, and must have lived in the United States for nine years—two longer than for the House. "The propriety of these distinctions is explained by the nature of the senatorial trust," wrote Madison. Not only does such a post require more life experience, but its confidential quality demands candidates who are "thoroughly weaned from the prepossessions and habits incident to foreign birth and education."[168]

Fourthly, the deliberative character of the Senate calls for a permanency that would be inappropriate for the House. The Founders recognized that Senators must be able to attend to such weighty matters as managing foreign relations or reviewing justices for the bench without having to fret about frequent reelections. For this reason they decided to assign Senators a term of six years, and in order to prevent wholesale turnover all at the same time also decreed that a third of the body run for reelection every two years. However, concern for the Senate's responsibilities was not the Founders' only motivation for stabilizing it in this way. They viewed the Senate as a vital counterbalance for the House of Representatives. As the Senate and the House work side by side, each body's structure and

---

168   *Ibid.*, 313.

operation complements the other, keeping them both in place and preserving the sovereignty of the people.

The Executive Branch

Although Congress exercises significant power, the Founders arranged for its influence to be effective only in cooperation with the second branch: the executive. As the name implies, the executive's primary responsibility is to execute and enforce the laws passed by the legislature. According to Article II, Section 1, of the Constitution, executive power is embodied in the office of the President of the United States. The President's duties are both domestic and international. Internally, he implements laws with the assistance of his cabinet, serves as Commander-in-Chief of the armed forces, nominates judges and ambassadors, and recommends legislation to Congress. Externally, he acts as America's representative to the rest of the world. He is responsible for drafting treaties, conducting foreign negotiations, and receiving foreign ministers.

While the relationship between the House and Senate provoked the most controversy within the Constitutional Convention, the issue perhaps that produced the greatest *fear* among the people was the extent of executive power. Traditionally, Americans tended to be suspicious of politically ambitious individuals. This attitude was so exacerbated by their experience with British royalty that, by the time of the Revolution, many Americans despised anything that even hinted at monarchy.

However, after securing their independence from

King George, Americans slowly began to realize the necessity
of establishing some form of executive power. The Articles of
Confederation had vested all power in the national legislature,
making no practical provision for the implementation of its laws.
The result was disastrous. Lacking an authoritative, unifying force,
the 13 states became hostile to each other. Congress was powerless
to enforce law or defend the country and consequently failed to
command any respect abroad. The members of the Constitutional
Convention took this lesson to heart but had difficulty deciding what
form the executive branch should take. Should the office be held
by one person or more? What should be its mode of appointment?
Should the office be held for life or limited by terms?

A popular idea at the time of the Convention was that
the executive should consist of two or more persons, similar to the
Roman Republic and its consuls. Proponents of this argument based
their reasoning on the same principle applied in the legislature, in
which the division of power acted as a safeguard against tyranny.
However, Alexander Hamilton suggested that the most important
quality for such a position was "dispatch" or energy. The duties
of waging war, defending the nation and conducting confidential
negotiations required the executive to act quickly and effectively.
While a proper division in the legislature tended to strengthen the
quality of its proceedings, division in the executive branch would
be a great weakness, compromising the nation's security. "A feeble
executive implies a feeble execution of government," Hamilton
argued. "A feeble execution is but another phrase for a bad execution:

And a government ill executed, whatever it may be in theory, must be in practice a bad government."[169]

If the executive consists of a single person, protested Hamilton's opponents, who or what shall provide a check on his power? Without an equal and opposing force, such an individual could easily become a tyrant. On the contrary, replied Hamilton, the very fact that he retains all power within himself will be check enough on the executive. "[O]ne of the weightiest objections to a plurality in the executive," wrote Hamilton, "is that it tends to conceal faults, and destroy responsibility."[170] If executive power is confined to an individual, that individual alone must answer to the people for his use of that power. The greater the weight of his office, the more will he be compelled to discharge his duties with honor.[171]

This reasoning led to a second argument concerning the nature of executive appointment. Certain members of the Constitutional Convention had suggested Congress ought to choose the executive in order to keep the latter dependent upon the legislature for his authority. Hamilton disagreed with this logic, declaring that such dependency would destroy the whole point behind separating the two powers. Instead, he argued, "the sense of the people should operate in the choice of the person to whom so important a trust [is] to be confided." While some delegates supported Hamilton's argument, others worried that the people would be inclined, at various times, to elect a demagogue or another unqualified individual simply because he

---

169   Alexander Hamilton, *Federalist 70*, 355.
170   *Ibid.*, 358.
171   *Ibid.*, 359-360.

stirred their passion. This concern sparked a complicated debate, after which the members emerged with an intricate but workable plan for executive appointment.

Article II, Section 1 of the Constitution describes the formation and duties of what has come to be called the *Electoral College*. The people of each state would select a group of experienced and learned men (excepting those currently serving in public office), amounting to the number of officials representing the state in Congress. These groups were to gather within their respective states to compile a list of persons deemed fit for office. Each elector was allowed to cast two votes, one of which had to be for a candidate from outside the state. After voting, the electors were to send a record of their ballots to the U.S. Senate. Once the Senate gathered votes from the electors, the head of the assembly would read aloud the ballots during session. If any one candidate received a majority of votes, calculated according to the number of electors, he would be named president of the United States. In the event of a tie, or if no candidate received a majority, the House of Representatives would vote by state for the executive, each state having one vote. After selecting the president, the candidate with the second highest number of votes was to be named vice president.

Though the system was complex, the Founders believed the design to be a healthy medium between the sovereignty of the people and the power of the legislature. As a body created for a specific purpose and for a specified length of time, the Electoral College would be free of all competing interests. "[T]he appointment of the president," wrote Hamilton, "[will not] depend on any pre-existing bodies of men who might be tampered with before hand to prostitute their votes." Instead, the election will be "an immediate act of the people of America, to be exerted in the choice of persons for the temporary and sole purpose of making the appointment." In addition, the requirement that the college meet by state instead of in a single convention greatly decreased the possibility of corruption from the outside. After all, Hamilton reminded his readers, the "business of corruption, when it is to embrace so considerable a number of men, requires time, as well as means."

It is now a common belief among many, if not most, Progressives, that the Electoral College is a vestige of the slaveholders who put our republic in place and as such should be done away with, replaced purely by the national popular vote; in short, pure democracy. This entire mentality and approach is based on ignorance as to why the Founders' created the Electoral College, but also what the Electoral College seeks to accomplish and prevent. The Founders did not want "regionalism" or "sectionalism" to triumph; that is, they did not want a candidate, or candidates, from a certain region dominating national elections. *Without* the Electoral College, large populations of voters concentrated in large cities and populous states would always choose the President. *With* the Electoral College, there must be broad support for a candidate to actually win the Presidency.

The Electoral College was another manifestation of the Founders deep loathing of pure democracy: They did not believe in it, feared it, and wanted to build into the republic as many mechanisms and structures to prevent pure democracy from ever taking hold inside the United States. They did not trust the American people to *not* give in to the allure of pure democracy, which would lead to mob rule, because again, they did not trust imperfect human nature.

Yet more importantly, the Founders did not trust themselves: The men in Philadelphia were the leading men of the day. They were not ignorant of the fact that many of them would be members of the government they were proposing: They would be the Representatives, the Senators, the Judges, and the Presidents of the envisioned American Republic. But instead of creating a system that would have benefited them and the potential to wield great, consolidated power, the men forming our government intentionally put in place the mechanisms that would restrict them and diffuse the power many of them would soon be wielding. This is one of the great testaments of who these imperfect men were: An acknowledgement of their own imperfections and shortcomings and the building of safeguards against their own human nature.

After settling the mode of appointment, the Founders debated the length of time an executive should be permitted to serve. Suggestions varied from allowing the executive to serve for life to limiting him to a one-time term of only several months. They settled, finally, on a presidential term of four years, judging the duration long enough to attract the interest of talented statesmen and brief enough to keep the office accountable to the people. Though some argued vehemently that each president be limited to one term only,

Hamilton declared that re-eligibility would be healthy for the office. "[T]he best security for the fidelity of mankind is to make their interest coincide with their duty," he said.[172] If the president were restricted to only one term in office, asked Hamilton, what incentive would he have to discharge his duties honorably? None but his own virtue, which cannot wholly be depended upon, even in the best of men. But if it remains possible that the people might return him to power, the executive will be that much more eager to please them through excellent service.

The Judicial Branch

In establishing separate branches for the legislative and executive functions of government, the authors of the Constitution were improving upon an old idea. In England, the ancient relationship between King and Parliament had hinted at this concept, but the two powers had never fully separated from each other. The Founding Fathers had studied this pattern carefully and had successfully completed this separation in the American government. But after this accomplishment, they designed a true innovation in adding a third branch to the government: the judiciary.

Many years prior to the American Revolution, Montesquieu had noted in his writings the need for all free governments to maintain a "depository" for the laws of the land. The legislature enacted law and the executive enforced it, but who was to ensure that these two powers never rose above it? Montesquieu's question was

---

172   *Ibid., Federalist 72, 367.*

answered by the institution of the American judiciary.[173]

The judicial branch of the United States government is the least defined of the three. Article III, Section 1 of the Constitution simply reads that the "Judicial power of the United States, shall be vested in one supreme court, and in such inferior courts as the Congress may, from time to time, ordain and establish." When the judicial branch was first constructed, Alexander Hamilton declared that branch to be "beyond comparison" the feeblest division of the national government. "The judiciary . . . has no influence over either the sword or the purse," he wrote, "no direction either of the strength or of the wealth of the society. . . . It may truly be said to have neither Force nor Will, but merely judgment."[174]

The judicial branch, and particularly the Supreme Court, has no direct historical precedent. It is a unique American feature to a constitutional republic. At its inception, it remained to be seen how the judiciary would exert its authority. The Founders' intention in establishing the Supreme Court was to create a body whose sole interest was to protect the original intent of the Constitution. "[E]very government ought to possess the means of executing its own provision by its own authority," declared Alexander Hamilton.[175] The Court, he said, "owing its official existence to the union, will never be likely to feel any bias inauspicious to the principles on which it is founded."[176] Thus, dependent neither on Congress nor the states, the Court is qualified to judge all cases of national import

---

173   Kirk, 356.
174   Hamilton, *Federalist 78*, 393–394.
175   *Ibid.*, *Federalist 80*, 405. Original "ought … authority" is italicized.
176   *Ibid.*

or those involving one or more states. In addition, it maintains jurisdiction over all cases regarding ambassadors, foreign powers, maritime law, disputes between states, and any accusation of treason.

The legal sovereignty exercised by the Supreme Court does promote national unity in that it sets a single standard for all of the states. De Tocqueville commended the Supreme Court as an effective arbiter between America's "two rival governments," the national administration and the network of state legislatures.[177] But in practice, the authority granted to the Court on paper has expanded far beyond this description. Because the Court answers only to the Constitution, it has the power of judicial review, or the authority to declare void any federal or state law that it judges to be inconsistent with that document. Given that the Court lacks an official check on its authority, Congress and the state legislatures are forced to rely on the virtue and sound judgment of those populating the bench.[178] The chief external influence exercised over the Court occurs in the appointment of justices. The President is responsible for nominating judges to the federal court; his choices must be approved by the Senate before nominees assume office. While the Constitution does

---

177   de Tocqueville, 108. Tocqueville writes: "But as it was foreseen that …
questions could arise relative to the exact limits of this [federal] government … [the
Founders] created a high federal court, a unique tribunal, one attribute of which
was to maintain the division of power between the two rival governments as the
Constitution had established it."

178   The Constitution does not explicitly delegate the power of judicial review.
Hamilton, an ardent federalist, strongly supported it in Federalist 78, stating that
the court's "duty [is] to declare all acts contrary to the manifest tenor of the Constitution void" (394). The Anti-Federalists objected, believing that this power should
belong to the state legislatures. The matter remained controversial until the Supreme
Court sanctioned judicial review in *Marbury v. Madison* (1803).

not set a time limit on how long federal judges can serve, upon taking the bench, justices are permitted to serve for life, or "during good behaviour."[179] The Founders granted the members of the Court this unusual privilege out of concern for their independence and strength of will. Hamilton stated that an "inflexible and uniform adherence to the rights of the constitution and of individuals . . . can certainly not be expected from judges who hold their offices by a temporary commission." Hamilton also argued that permanency would allow justices to devote themselves wholly to the study of the law, a practice essential for accurate judgments.[180]

Despite the care with which they designed the Constitution, the Founding Fathers recognized that the preservation of the new system would require more than ink on parchment. No man could be trusted to keep the law by sheer willpower. Instead, to act lawfully, he must be motivated by an external force, by the restrictions and boundaries of the machinery of a republic. James Madison believed that this principle was the key to keeping the three branches of government within their constitutional boundaries. If the ambition of each branch is fixed in opposition to the others, he said, no one branch will be able to dominate. "[T]he great security against a gradual concentration of the several powers in the same department," wrote Madison, "consists in giving to those who administer each department the necessary constitutional means, and personal motives, to resist encroachments of the others. . . . Ambition must be

---

179   *U.S. Constitution*, Art. III, Sec. 1. The Constitution provides impeachment as the vehicle of removal for insurgent judges.

180   Hamilton, *Federalist 78*, 398-399.

made to counteract ambition."[181]

To put it another way, every human being has self-interests; that is basic human nature. Governments, associations—all are comprised of human beings with self-interests who usually align themselves with others who have the same priorities. What must be done in a constitutional republic is to guarantee that there is not too much concentration of power put in place and that there are mechanisms by which self-interest counteracts self-interest. The first step that the Founders took toward this goal was to separate from each other the powers to *make* law, *enforce* law, and *interpret* law. The second step was to mingle the powers of one branch with another, forcing all three to operate together as a unit. An example of this intermingling is the executive power of veto. Every proposal passed by Congress, before it becomes law, must be sent to the President for his approval. Every bill he favors he signs into law, but those to which he objects he returns to Congress unsigned, accompanied by an explanation of his disapproval. If Congress wishes to override the veto, each house must pass the bill by at least two-thirds.

De Tocqueville praised the wisdom of this provision in limiting the power of Congress. "[The] dependence of the executive power [upon the legislature] is one of the vices inherent in republican constitutions," he wrote. "The Americans were not able to destroy the inclination that brings legislative assemblies to take hold of the government, but they rendered this inclination less irresistible."[182]

Although the basic structure which the Founders established

---

181   Madison, *Federalist 51*, 262.
182   de Tocqueville, 114.

remains in place, the American government has undergone many significant changes over the years. Our complex yet unified system does not operate as it once did. Various reforms, such as the 17th Amendment, the Supreme Court acting as a super legislature, Congress and the states abdicating power—all of these have caused us to drift from the Founders' original intent.

CHAPTER THIRTEEN
The Transformation of the Concept of 'Rights'

———————◆———————

"Administrative centralization, it is true, succeeds at uniting at a given period and in a certain place all the disposable strength of the nation," wrote de Tocqueville, "but it is harmful to the reproduction of strength. . . . It can therefore contribute admirably to the passing greatness of one man, not to the lasting prosperity of a people."[183]

The Civil War

For several decades following the American Founding, the states enjoyed a significant degree of independence from the federal government. Each state jealously guarded its unique heritage and identity, and state legislatures handled most of their affairs without any assistance from the central administration. However, there was a single controversy which had simmered within the national consciousness even prior to the Revolution: *slavery*. By the mid-19th century, the issue of black slavery had pushed its way to the surface,

---

183   *Ibid*, 83.

sharply dividing the northern and southern states.

The many differences that developed between the North and South concerning slavery and its vital role in the southern economy eventually exploded into the American Civil War (1861-1865). A full analysis of the causes, events, and consequences of the war is worthy of its own book. What cannot be ignored, however, is how the war began a process that fundamentally altered the federal government and the public's perception of national leadership.

In 1865, the states adopted the 13th Amendment to the Constitution, outlawing slavery and "involuntary servitude."[184] However, during the dark days of Reconstruction, southern communities treated the newly freed blacks with contempt, passing legislation meant to keep them separate from and subordinate to whites. These Black Codes, as they were called, effectively denied blacks the rights belonging to American citizens.

In response to the Black Codes, Congress proceeded in 1868 to pass the 14th Amendment to protect blacks from political and social persecution. The amendment stated: "All persons born or naturalized in the United States, and subject to the jurisdiction thereof, are citizens of the United States and of the State wherein they reside." Furthermore, it declared that "[n]o State shall make or enforce any law which shall abridge the privileges or immunities of citizens of the United States; nor shall any State deprive any person of life, liberty, or property, without due process of law; nor deny to any person within its jurisdiction the equal protection of the laws."

---

184   The amendment specifies that slavery is acceptable only "as a punishment for crime whereof the party shall have been duly convicted...."

When the 14th Amendment was adopted, its intentions seemed clear. Each clause addressed a specific problem and offered a specific remedy. The clause regarding "privileges and immunities" declared that all American citizens, regardless of race, must not be denied their fundamental rights, such as the right to vote, the right to own property, and the right to trial by jury. The provision of "due process of law" guaranteed that no responsible citizen would be deprived of his rights, and "equal protection" guarded free citizens from unjust or discriminatory legislation.[185]

At the time of its passage, the 14th Amendment was in no way intended to establish *new* rights or privileges for the American people, but simply to extend *existing* rights to those who had been denied them. In fact, the amendment was not meant to be an "active" law at all, but was designed to prevent unlawful treatment of blacks. Americans at this time never expected the federal government to make laws binding on the states except those pertaining to national interests or the fundamental rights of all the people. All other legislative power belonged to the states. Most legislative activity from the Founding era until the end of the 19th century was meant to keep the central administration at bay instead of soliciting its involvement in the community.

Constitutional historian Raoul Berger explains that the traditional American attitude toward the federal government has almost always been one of apprehension:

---

185   Raoul Berger, *Government by Judiciary: The Transformation of the Fourteenth Amendment*, 2nd ed. (Indianapolis: Liberty Fund, 1997), 18.

Historically the citizenry have relied upon the States for
protection, and such protection was afforded before
the Constitutional Convention by a Bill of Rights in
virtually every state Constitution. It was not fear of
State misgovernment but distrust of the remote federal
newcomer that fueled the demand for a federal Bill of
Rights. . . . This was understood by the framers of the
Fourteenth Amendment, and their own attachment
to State sovereignty led them to refrain from intruding
beyond the ban on discrimination against blacks with
respect to certain rights.[186]

However, not long after the 14th Amendment was passed,
some began to argue that the amendment made the Bill of Rights
applicable to the *states*, a doctrine that would become known as
incorporation. In 1873, for example, the Supreme Court heard the
Slaughterhouse Cases, in which a guild of butchers in New Orleans
protested against a local slaughterhouse corporation that had been
granted a monopoly by the state. The butchers argued that the
state was violating the Fifth Amendment by depriving them of
their property without due process of law. They grounded their
argument on the basis that the 14th Amendment prohibited a state
from abridging the "privileges and immunities" of its citizens. The
Supreme Court rejected this argument, responding that the Bill of
Rights was intended to limit the federal government from interfering
with state law.[187] Despite this resolution, the Court began to soften

---

186   *Ibid.*, 156.
187   *The Slaughterhouse Cases*, 16 Wall. (83 U.S.) 36, 21 L.Ed. 394 (1873).

its position over the years as attorneys persisted in bringing similar arguments before the bench.

In 1923, a New Yorker by the name of Benjamin Gitlow was arrested for coordinating the distribution of Communist literature. In *Gitlow v. New York*, the state Supreme Court convicted Gitlow of criminal anarchy, a decision which was subsequently affirmed by the appellate court. When Gitlow appealed to the United States Supreme Court, the bench upheld the lower court's decision. However, the Court added a significant twist to its ruling. While reviewing the case, the Court declared that the First Amendment right to free speech was protected from infringement by the states under the due process clause of the 14th Amendment, and that Gitlow could be convicted only because he "[advocated] the overthrow of organized government by force, violence and unlawful means."[188] While seemingly innocuous, the carefully crafted ruling opened the door for judicial activism in the future.

In 1965, the Supreme Court heard *Griswold v. Connecticut*, a case regarding a Connecticut state law that prohibited medical practitioners from recommending or providing contraceptives to their patients. The law had been challenged by the state chapter of Planned Parenthood, which insisted that the statute was unconstitutional. In a vote of seven to two, the justices ruled that the Connecticut law violated citizens' "right to privacy." The Court argued that this "right," though nowhere mentioned in the Constitution, is suggested by the First, Third, Fifth and Ninth

---

188   *Gitlow v. People of the State of New York*, 268 U.S. 652 (1925).

Amendments and is therefore protected under the Fourteenth.[189] This legal invention not only paved the way for the full incorporation of the Bill of Rights but also set a notorious precedent for other controversial cases, including *Roe v. Wade* (1973).

The Progressive Era: The Birth of the Leviathan

Writing to an associate in 1788, Thomas Jefferson remarked, "the natural progress of things is for liberty to yield and government to gain ground."[190] How true this is, especially when the people allow it to happen. It seems ironic today that one of the most intense debates over the ratification of the Constitution was the question of whether or not it gave the federal government too much power. The bitter conflict between the Federalists, who favored a strong federal government, and the Anti-Federalists, who argued that centralized power would threaten the rights of states and individual citizens, almost torpedoed the entire constitutional movement.

However, in 21st-century America, we the people not only allow the government into some of our most intimate spaces, we actually invite it in. We still talk a great deal about our "rights," but our understanding of those rights has changed. Historically, Americans understood their individual rights to be boundary markers, showing where the government was not to intrude into their lives. But over time, we have come to treat rights as claims on

---

189   *Griswold v. Connecticut*, 391 U.S. 86 S. Ct. 1678 (1965).

190   Thomas Jefferson, *Letter to Edward Carrington*, May 27, 1788. Buckner F. Melton, Jr. ed., The Quotable Founding Fathers (New York: Fall River Press, 2004), 142.

the government—as the "things," great or small, that the government is supposed to give us. Instead of demanding that the government stay within its constitutional boundaries, we welcome it where it was never meant to go.

This transformation in our thinking took root in the 19th century and accelerated in the 20th, fueled by some of the most dramatic social and political changes in American history. Led by the educated, a broad-based social movement emerged, attracting the poor, oppressed, and disillusioned. Eloquent rhetoricians and writers began training the American people to look to the federal government to help them, advocate for them and provide for them: the Progressive Movement was born.

In the 1880s, the United States, eager to crawl out of the rubble of the Civil War, entered a period of remarkable economic growth and prosperity. American innovation, combined with the country's seemingly infinite natural resources, provided unprecedented opportunities for amassing wealth. The railroad industry exploded, bringing with it the ability to carry passengers and goods from coast to coast. European immigrants—some 20 million between 1880 and 1920 —crowded to American shores in search of a new life, flooding the market with cheap labor. The immigrants brought new cultures, traditions, and loyalties that forever altered the American social and political landscape.

As mass immigration was transforming American society, companies merged into corporations, and corporations developed into trusts.[191] Wealthy "robber barons" manipulated the market to their advantage and frequently exchanged favors and kick-backs with unethical politicians. Industrial tycoons developed close relationships with government insiders, and together they formed corrupt but immensely powerful political machines. Gradually, as the government endured a series of incompetent or weak-willed presidential administrations, powerful businessmen began to virtually control national economic policy. While they abused some of their power and wealth, the point is not to condemn the ingenious, risk-taking individuals who helped lead the nation into great prosperity. It is to condemn the fact that they joined with corrupt politicians to increase their power, manipulate the system of government, and maximize their wealth at the expense of competition. They were not truly interested in a competitive, free market. They were interested in creating a system of crony capitalism, a system that was to their benefit and not necessarily to the people as a whole.

As power and wealth increased, unfortunately so did opportunities for corruption. Politicians at both the state and federal level were willing to pull strings for big businesses in order to benefit themselves. As the rich grew more powerful, the system of government became imbalanced, no longer neutral and began to emphasize the interests of the wealthy elite because they had captured the power of government to promote their own interests. As a natural response, the working classes' interests were ignored,

---

191   Paul Johnson, *A History of the American People* (New York: HarperPerennial, 1997), 561.

and they sank deeper into oppression. Fair labor standards, the rights of workers regarding pay, and safety standards in work environments were dismissed because the government sided with the wealthy. Workers and their families, driven by the need for work, many times came to urban areas and ended up in less than ideal living situations. The deepening class disparity and its incumbent social concerns sparked debate and protests across the country. Left-leaning, educated activists began forming a new political philosophy that they believed would mitigate class oppression. The Progressive movement came out of this economic and societal upheaval and developed into a broad-based social development. Over time, while their ideas and actions were confronting real societal injustices, they would prove to be an overcorrection.

It was a movement that in many ways was birthed inside the Republican Party by the likes of Wisconsin's Robert La Follette, who decried this "unholy alliance" between business and government.[192] The Progressive movement agreed with most Americans that everyone—the worker as well as the business owner—should have a fair opportunity to succeed. The Progressives, however, argued that a truly democratic government should not just protect equal opportunities, but should also be empowered to step in and regulate business practices and social conditions as necessary in order to guarantee equal opportunity to all. But no matter how much that was their desire, what they ultimately argued for was government

---

192   Theodore Roosevelt, *"Platform of the Progressive Party,"* 7 August 1912. In this speech, Roosevelt declared that, "to dissolve the unholy alliance between corrupt business and corrupt politics is the first task of the statesmanship of the day."

control of business to tip the scales in favor of labor and Progressive ideas at the expense of the free market and competition. The fundamental problem and overcorrection of Progressives was this: out of government intervention to guarantee equal opportunity came the next logical step that there must be government intervention to guarantee equal outcomes.

As Progressive writer Herbert Croly (1869-1930), also a Republican and one of the first to articulate Progressive ideologies, wrote: "[The] democratic state should never discriminate in favor of anything or anybody. [The state] should only discriminate against all sorts of privilege. . . . [P]opular government is to make itself expressly and permanently responsible for the amelioration of the individual and society. . . ."[193] Croly insisted that the only way for America to achieve true social equality was for the government to direct the nation's resources towards that end.

Though Progressives did not advocate the eradication of individual interests, they did believe that government should be responsible for molding such interests to promote the general welfare. With echoes of Rousseau's concept of the general will, Croly would write that "Individual freedom is important, but more important still is the freedom of a whole people to dispose of its own destiny."[194] Whether Croly did not understand, or would not admit, was that with this statement he sought to obliterate individual freedom.

Progressive philosophy began to inspire various reforms,

---

193   Hebert Croly, *The Promise of American Life* (New York: Macmillan, 1909). See Chapter 7.
194   *Ibid.*

many of them pertaining to elections. The Progressives successfully campaigned for a constitutional amendment that would take the power of electing U.S. senators out of the hands of state legislatures and put it into the hands of the people. The 17th Amendment was designed to end the "cozy" relationship between big money and state politicos, specifically party bosses dictating senatorial picks to state legislators, by requiring senators to respond directly to the voter base. But what it did was actually bring us closer to direct democracy. Progressives also introduced the idea of direct primaries. During this period, political parties had enormous leeway in determining which candidates were nominated for public office. The direct primary, instituted as a way of returning this influence to the people, permitted the voters themselves to whittle down the choice of candidates for the general election. Progressives also changed the actual ballots in use for elections. For decades, Americans used a variety of balloting methods in their elections. Powerful local interests and political parties often used these methods to their advantage. It was common practice for party officials to provide voters with "pre-packaged" ballots that listed only the party's candidates. Progressives fought successfully for a slate of rules to regulate balloting that would eliminate all undue influences on voters. One result was the implementation of the Australian ballot, otherwise known as the secret ballot. As the term *Australian* implies, it was first used in Australia, but its use quickly spread around the globe. This ballot, which was completely secret, listed all candidates running for office and was handed out by official poll workers, not party activists.[195] It would first be adopted in the United States in the 1888 elections, achieving widespread use in the early 20th century as Progressives pushed ballot reform to continue breaking the power of the party bosses.

While these reforms addressed some genuine problems in the election process, they also introduced new problems. The 17th Amendment unwittingly threw off the built-in balance of the federal system. As previously discussed, state legislatures had been given the power to elect senators in order to provide a "check" on both the federal government and the shifting winds of public opinion as represented by the House of Representatives as well as popular opinion in Washington, DC. With the 17th Amendment, the states' power of accountability and real representation in Washington was greatly diminished. The federal government was suddenly elevated to a position of authority it had never enjoyed before. This change also opened the door for the federal government to oversee the day-to-day issues affecting citizens. State and local governments began to take even more subservient roles. And while direct primaries and secret ballots may have curbed party power, they also eliminated the parties' ability to hold elected officials accountable for their actions: The average tenure of a congressman in the 1880s was three years. It's now nine years, and as we have seen with many Senators in recents times, their careers can span decades in that chamber.

As the Progressive mindset began to permeate American society, the general public became more and more comfortable seeing

---

195   John L. Moore, *Elections A to Z* (Washington, DC: Congressional Quarterly Inc., 1999)

the federal government as a guardian who could solve all social ills. And if the federal government was going to solve all social ills, it had to be a well-endowed, well-oiled machine. People began to see bureaucracy as a sign of health and efficiency: The more bureaucracy, the healthier the society. Politicians, who stood to benefit from a powerful, centralized government, encouraged this line of thinking.

In 1912, Theodore Roosevelt lost the Republican party nomination to William Taft, so he left the party and campaigned for reelection under the Progressive Bull Moose Party banner. Though Roosevelt ultimately lost to Democrat Woodrow Wilson, the election was an overwhelming triumph for the Progressives.[196] Wilson, formerly president of Princeton University and Governor of New Jersey, not only believed that the government was responsible for promoting the public interest, but he also had great confidence in the government's ability to determine and accomplish what was best for American citizens.

To Wilson, the government was not a necessary evil but a benevolent figure, and he expressed these views during his presidential campaign. While stumping in Scranton, Pennsylvania, where he addressed a group of miners, Wilson stressed the government's need—and right—to regulate industry. He referred to the U.S. Bureau of Mines as a "foster father of the miners of the United States," whose job it was "to see that the life of human beings

---

196   Taft, the Republican Party candidate and White House incumbent, walked away with only eight electoral votes. Wilson, Roosevelt, and Socialist Party candidate Eugene Debs—all representatives of the political left—together won a remarkable 75 percent of the popular vote. See Sidney M. Milkis and Michael Nelson, The American Presidency: Origins and Development, 1776-2002, 4th ed. (Washington, DC: CQ Press, 2003), 230.

[in this case, miners] was . . . safeguarded."[197]

Wilson's election and administration (1913-1921) reflected a fundamental change in popular thought. Historian Paul Johnson describes this change, referring to Wilson's presidency as "one of the great watersheds of American history":

> Until this time, America had concentrated almost exclusively on developing its immense natural resources by means of a self-creating and self-recruiting meritocracy. Americans enjoyed a laissez-faire society which was by no means unrestrained but whose limitations to their economic freedom were imposed by their belief in a God-ordained moral code rather than a government devised by man. . . . [But gradually] the progressive intelligentsia . . . began to see a strong federal government, with wide powers of intervention, as the defender of the ordinary man and woman against the excesses of corporate power.[198]

A significant aspect of this watershed was the reformation in the way that the people perceived their rights. Before Wilson's time, as previously mentioned, Americans viewed their rights as claims *against* government, but under Progressive influence they began to perceive them as claims *on* government. This transition in how Americans viewed their government cannot be stressed strongly enough. This transformation was borne out most dramatically in

---

197   Woodrow Wilson, *"Campaign Address in Scranton, Penn.,"* September 23, 1912, accessed at http://teachingamericanhistory.org/library/index. asp?document-print=446.
198   Johnson, 627, 636.

the public's reinterpretation of the Bill of Rights. For example, Americans had originally understood the Fourth Amendment's provision that no citizen would "be deprived of life, liberty, or property, without due process of law," as a restriction on the federal government, forbidding it from exercising unlawful authority. This is why many still believe that the federal government should have verifiable evidence before surveilling private citizens. To not do so is a gross violation of the Fourth Amendment and civil liberties and is deeply unconstitutional.

However, when the Progressive era redefined "rights," the public began to view the Fourth Amendment as an obligation upon government to provide them with life, liberty, and property. This fundamental shift in thinking influenced many Americans' views of government and rights moving forward.

Once in power, the Wilson administration and its Democrat Congress set to work reforming the government itself. In 1913, they prevailed upon the states to adopt two new amendments to the Constitution. The first was the 16th Amendment, which established federal income tax. The government justified the tax by claiming that it would need the revenue to act as an effective guardian of the people. They also believed the tax would narrow the socioeconomic gap between the corporate man and the common man.[199] The second amendment was, of course, the 17th, which transferred Senate elections from the state legislatures to the people. While the main purpose of this change was to break the power of corrupt

---

199   *Ibid.*, 624, 636-637.

party bosses, it should be noted that the Democrat Party did so for self-serving reasons: They anticipated that votes from the common people would ensure its Congressional majority for years to come.

In 1914, the newly empowered federal government pursued an interventionist agenda, establishing the Federal Trade Commission to closely regulate business practices, and passing the Clayton Antitrust Act to break up corporate monopolies. As the central government assumed more responsibility, it created more federal departments and offices and infiltrated more areas of daily life. The government was rapidly fulfilling one of Wilson's own campaign statements: "[I]n these great beehives [of society] where in every corridor swarm men of flesh and blood it is . . . the privilege of the government . . . to see that human life is properly cared for and that the human lungs have something to breathe."[200]

Wilson believed government should play a role in monitoring not only business practices but also human behavior and relationships. Using the metaphor of a benign "patrolman" with a lamp, Wilson indicated that government, in the hands of the right people, should go "through all the passages of the beehive in which we live, and see to it that men are remaining our neighbors and doing their duty as human beings."[201] In short, Wilson believed government should be Big Brother.

The New Deal

Wilson's second term in office, however, was troubled by

---

200   Wilson, *"The Meaning of Democracy."*
201   *Ibid.*

recession and the advent of World War I. In 1920, the people elected to the presidency Warren G. Harding, a Republican who eventually reversed the economic slump by slashing federal spending.[202] Throughout the '20s, Americans continued to elect presidents whose *laissez-faire* policies paved the way for unprecedented prosperity during the decade. Calvin Coolidge, who would follow Harding, would represent the last President to not succumb to Progressive tendencies, and he oversaw a period of great American prosperity. But during Herbert Hoover's Administration, this boom was reversed by a complex series of events, culminating in the stock market crash of 1929 and the onset of the Great Depression. The resulting poverty and unemployment caused the American people to lose faith in the free market. Trained by progressives to demand economic and social remedies and intervention from Government, the people began pleading with their national leaders for help.[203]

In 1932 the Democrat Governor of New York, Franklin D. Roosevelt, ran for President, saying that the time had come for a "re-appraisal of values."[204] He believed that it was the government's responsibility to adapt its practices to the needs of each generation. "The task of statesmanship," he declared, "has always been the re-

---

202   Johnson, 708. Johnson comments: "Harding inherited from the comatose Wilson regime one of the sharpest recessions in American history. By July 1921 it was all over and the economy was booming again. Harding and [Treasury Secretary Andrew] Mellon had done nothing except cut government expenditure by a huge 40 percent from Wilson's peacetime level, the last time a major industrial power treated a recession by classic laissez-faire methods...."

203   Jeffrey E. Cohen, *Politics and Economic Policy in the United States*, 2nd ed. (Boston: Houghton Mifflin, 2000), 49.

204   Franklin D. Roosevelt, *"The Commonwealth Club Address (1932),"* in Dolbeare and Cummings, 410.

definition of . . . rights in terms of a changing and growing social order." Roosevelt blamed the Depression on the government's indulgence of special interests, particularly those of the business community. "Should [big business] ever use its collective power contrary to public welfare," he claimed, "the Government must be swift to enter and protect the public interest." Roosevelt promised that, if elected President, he would see to it that government restored the economy and ensured to everyone the "right to make a comfortable living."[205]

Roosevelt won the election with almost 90 percent of the electoral vote. In office, he began implementing what he called the "New Deal," a series of federal projects meant to rescue the country from recession. Through the New Deal, Roosevelt enabled the federal government to assume responsibilities that exceeded even Progressive Era expectations. While Progressives had been content for the government to regulate market activity, Roosevelt enacted policies to artificially stimulate market growth. He appointed dozens of new boards and agencies to oversee existing industries and to supervise new ones. Under his leadership, the government began to insure bank deposits, supervise the Stock Exchange, restrict competition in various industries, and even fix rates for railroad travel.[206]

All of these actions corresponded with Roosevelt's vision for American government: "[T]o help make the system of free

---

205 *Ibid.*
206 Jeffrey E. Cohen, *Politics and Economic Policy in the United States*, 2nd ed. (Boston: Houghton Mifflin, 2000), 49-50.

enterprise work, to provide that minimum security without which the competitive system cannot function, [and] to restrain the kind of individual action which in the past has been harmful to the community."[207] Perhaps the most significant role assumed by the government during the New Deal was looking after the "social welfare." According to Roosevelt, the government was responsible for providing the people with "essential human freedoms," such as freedom from want or fear.[208] Accordingly, Roosevelt's administration invented programs such as the Works Progress Administration (WPA), meant to be temporary, which hired the unemployed to work on federally funded construction projects. Roosevelt also spearheaded the creation of the Social Security system as a way of securing insurance for the unemployed, the disadvantaged, and the retired. The system also loaned money to the states to be distributed to the poor.[209]

While these programs helped some people get back on their feet, they were not in fact temporary. They marked the beginnings of the welfare state, which would grow over time into the enormous system we have today. The government is always moving forward— growing in size, scale, and power. It does not—will not—restrict or limit itself of its own volition. Yet those who would restrain it will not either: In the decades since the New Deal, the American public has departed little from the Progressive mentality that

---

207   Franklin D. Roosevelt, "A Radio Address to the Young Democratic Clubs of America," August 24, 1935.
208   Roosevelt, "The Four Freedoms," delivered to the 77th Congress, January 6, 1941.
209   Johnson, 764.

people are "entitled" to government welfare. Today, Americans are being "trained" more than ever—through government-sponsored education, federal programs, and political rhetoric—to look to the government to meet their needs and fix their problems, big or small. Our representatives in Congress are happy to funnel massive amounts of federal funding to their constituents in order to win re-election. Since the American public has departed little from the Progressive mentality that people hold their rights as claims upon the government instead of as claims against it, this perspective continues to have significant implications on the role and activity of government today.

CHAPTER FOURTEEN
The Legislative Process: The Making of American Law

———◆———

"There is nothing more prolific in marvels than the art of being free; but there is nothing harder than the apprenticeship of freedom," wrote Alexis de Tocqueville. "Freedom . . . is ordinarily born in the midst of storms, it is established painfully among civil discords, and only when it is old can one know its benefits."[210]

The American legislative process is inarguably a laborious and time-consuming practice. Passing one piece of legislation may involve everyone from the lowliest citizen to the President of the United States, and may take years simply to reach the floor of Congress. Federal lawmakers struggle to please one special-interest group only to offend five others. Congress is often portrayed as a creature of partisanship and gridlock, and any given administration is accused of being everything from sinister to farcical. However, Americans often forget that each step of the multi-level legislative

---

210   de Tocqueville, 229.

process is an essential part of maintaining the freedom of our society.

Congressional Leadership

The basic leadership structure in Congress has changed little since the body first met in 1789. However, the activity and energy of each Congress can vary, depending on the personality of the leadership.

Congress is of course a bicameral or two-chamber body, consisting of the House of Representatives and the Senate. This division reflects the original tension in the Continental Congress between the large states, who wanted proportional representation, and the small states, who lobbied for equal representation. Thus, the House of Representatives contains 435 congressmen, each of whom represents a district in his or her state. Because districts are drawn according to population, currently for every 711,000 people, largely-populated states are represented by dozens of congressmen, while sparsely-populated states may have as few as one or two. The Senate, in contrast, contains only 100 senators—two from each of the 50 states. This design allows senators to exercise equal authority, regardless of the size of their states.

Both the House and Senate operate on a two-party system and have since the founding of political parties in this country. While there are numerous smaller political parties in the United States, it is the two major political parties, Democrat and Republican, that are the basis for real political power. Each chamber has a majority leader (or floor leader) who orchestrates the activities of the majority party. Likewise, the minority party also has a leader who looks after minority interests, and who works together with the majority leader to pass bipartisan legislation. Both majority and minority leaders keep a close eye on legislative activity in order to protect and advance their respective party agendas. In the House and Senate, both majority and minority leaders employ deputies or "whips" to rally members behind favorable bills or to mobilize them against harmful ones. Republicans and Democrats in both the House and Senate also maintain party *conferences* to keep their members organized and united behind the party platform.[211]

An office unique to the House of Representative is the Speaker of the House, whose position is prescribed in Article I, Section 2 of the Constitution.[212] Though the Speaker traditionally has a much lower profile than the President or Vice President, he, or she, wields a tremendous amount of authority and is a key player throughout the entire legislative process. As the highest-ranking official in the House, the Speaker is third in line to the presidency.[213] Elected by his or her fellow representatives at the beginning of each Congress, the Speaker serves as leader of the majority party and chief officer in charge of House activity. The Speaker determines the

---

211   Readers should note that House Democrats belong to the House Democratic Caucus; all other congressmen belong to conferences (i.e., House Republican Conference, Senate Republican Conference, and Senate Democratic Conference).

212   Though the Constitution does not require the Speaker to be a congressman, he always has been.

213   The Constitution grants Congress the power of "declaring what officer shall … act as president" in the event of both President and Vice President being unable to serve (Art. II, Sec. 1). In 1947, Congress passed the Presidential Succession Act, which officially appointed the Speaker of the House as third in line to the presidency.

legislative calendar, deciding which bills should come to the floor and when. If the Speaker disapproves of a bill for any reason, he or she may place it at the very end of the calendar, where it is likely to expire (all bills not considered by the end of the congressional term automatically "die" and must be reintroduced in a later session). The Speaker is responsible for appointing chairmen to the select committees, conference committees, and the Committee of the Whole (as the House is called when it forms itself into a committee). [214] One of the Speaker's most significant powers is that of assigning bills to one or more committees for consideration. The Speaker often uses this exclusive power strategically in order to expedite favorable legislation or to "kill" unfavorable legislation. During floor sessions, the Speaker recognizes other congressmen, rules on points of order, and directs the course of debate. As a representative, the Speaker may choose to step down from his or her seat temporarily, appointing another officer in his place, to participate in floor debates or to vote. However, in his or her official capacity, the Speaker may not cast a vote on the floor unless that vote is needed to break a tie.

Despite the breadth of these powers, today's Speaker of the House actually wields significantly less authority than many of his or her predecessors. When Congress was first established, few rules were placed on the Speaker's conduct, and only over time did representatives begin to realize the potential for official

---

214   Traditionally, Speakers assigned chairmanships according to seniority. But Speaker Newt Gingrich of the 104th Congress favored party loyalty over seniority in several of his committee appointments. His choices were part of the Republican plan to pass the "Contract with America" legislative package during the first 100 days of the congressional session. See Oleszek, 176 (following note).

abuse. In 1910, the House rebelled against the particularly iron-fisted rule of Speaker Joseph Cannon and revoked many of the Speaker's privileges, transferring some of his power to committee chairmen.[215]

The presiding officer in the Senate is the Vice President of the United States. The Vice President's most significant senatorial role is that of breaking the occasional tie. In his absence, floor activity is directed by the President *Pro Tempore* ("for a time"), a position traditionally assigned to the most senior member of the Senate.

Where Does a Bill Come From?

"There is nothing the human will despairs of attaining by the free action of the collective power of individuals," wrote de Tocqueville. "America is, among the countries of the world, the one where they have taken most advantage of association and where they have applied that powerful mode of action to a greater diversity of objects."[216]

De Tocqueville rightly discerned that in America, the legislative process is supposed to begin not in the halls of government but in American homes and communities. Traditionally, Americans have effected social or political change by forming groups or *associations* to voice their ideas. An association can be as small as a

---

215   Joseph G. Cannon, Speaker from 1903-1911, not only had power to appoint chairmen to all standing committees, but he also personally chaired the powerful Rules Committee. During the 1910 "revolt," the House removed the Speaker from the Rules Committee and limited his appointment powers to select committees and conference committees. See Roger H. Davidson and Walter J. Oleszek, Congress and Its Members, 7th ed. (Washington, DC: CQ Press, 2000), 166.
216   *Ibid.*, 180.

single neighborhood requesting the city council to repave their street or as large as a group of multi-million-dollar corporations petitioning Congress for regulatory reform. Today, formal associations are referred to as *special-interest groups*. Special-interests usually fall into one of four categories: economic, ideological (or policy-oriented), social and civil rights. Economic interest groups include labor and consumer rights advocates; ideological or policy-oriented groups include gun-control activists and organizations for or against abortion; social groups include veterans' organizations or disabled-rights advocates; and civil rights groups include proponents of African-American or women's rights.[217] An average American may belong to and participate in several such groups:

> Consider a hypothetical dairy farmer. The federal government is contemplating lowering dairy price supports and raising milk quality standards. The farmer expects the Farm Bureau, of which he is a member, to follow this matter closely through its Washington, DC office. A veteran of World War II, he also is a member of the American Legion, which is supporting a push in Congress to increase veterans' benefits. He attends a Lutheran church that is asking the governor to support the relaxation of the state's laws regulating charity raffles. Finally, he is a coach in the Little League and has signed a petition asking the town council to lower the speed limit next to the ballpark.[218]

---

217   James W. Ceaser, *American Government: Origins, Institutions and Public Policy*, 5th ed. (Dubuque, IA: Kendall/Hunt Publishing, 1998), 320-326.
218   *Ibid.*, 320.

Many special-interest groups hire *lobbyists* to attract lawmakers in support of their causes. Professional lobbyists advocate bills favorable to their cause and actively oppose legislation harmful to their interests. Lobbying may take on several different forms. *Direct lobbying* involves personal contact with legislators; professional lobbyists often visit congressional offices, attend committee meetings, and provide congressmen with up-to-date information on pertinent issues and make direct requests for action. *Social lobbying* is more informal, and may include socializing at parties or treating a potential ally to dinner.[219] On occasion, groups with divergent interests will join forces to lobby for a particular issue. This tactic is called *coalition lobbying*. During the 103rd Congress (1993-1994) for example, several traditionally opposed religious associations joined together to support the Religious Freedom Restoration Act. In recent years, *grassroots lobbying*, which generally solicits the support and involvement of ordinary citizens, has proven to be a very effective tool in influencing legislation. The Home School Legal Defense Association, for example, keeps homeschooling families informed on pending legislation at both state and federal levels, and helps members to contact their representatives by mail, phone, email, or social media. Together, special-interest groups and lobbyists generate a significant amount of the legislation that comes before Congress.[220]

---

219   Various rules and guidelines regulate the exchanging of gifts between lobbyists and legislators in order to discourage corruption.
220   Ceaser, 328-330.

One of Congress' most aggressive "lobbyists" is the President of the United States. As head of the Executive Branch, the President is responsible for working together with Congress to pass laws that are aligned with his administration's agenda that he can then implement. The Constitution states that the President, "shall from time to time give to the Congress information of the state of the union, and recommend to their consideration such measures as he shall judge necessary and expedient."[221] Today, the President gives this report in his annual State of the Union address, which until the beginning of the 20th century was typically sent in writing. Woodrow Wilson, in order to gain more support for his agenda items, felt that a personal address to Congress would be more powerful, thus beginning the tradition of the pomp and circumstance we see today. Since the beginning of the 20th century, Presidents have used this speech not only to make policy recommendations to Congress, but also to present to the legislature detailed agendas, or "blueprints," for their administrations. Executive agencies follow up on the President's speech by lobbying Congress to pass legislation and to fund their new initiatives.

Introducing a Bill

The actual draft of a bill might be written by a congressional committee, a Hill staffer, a lobbying firm, a member of an industry or even by an individual citizen. Government agencies, corporations and special-interest groups regularly employ attorneys to draft

---

221 *U.S. Constitution*, Art. II, Sec. 3.

legislation favorable to their agendas. Every congressman keeps a legislative counsel on staff to assist in writing bills. The President maintains an entire team of experts to draft legislation and assist in advancing his agenda.

Though virtually anyone may draft a bill, only a Congressman may formally introduce a bill in the House or Senate. In the House, a representative introduces a bill by placing it in the *hopper*, a box positioned on the clerk's desk at the front of the House chamber. In the Senate, where procedure is much less formal, a Senator may stand and personally introduce a bill. Once a bill is introduced, it is assigned a title and number. Bills originating in the House of Representatives are signified by the letters "HR"; those originating in the Senate are titled with "S." A bill's number indicates the timing of its introduction. For example, the title "H.R. 71" is assigned to the 71st bill introduced in the House during a given two-year session. Sometimes, sponsors seek out specific or distinguishing numbers for their bills. For example, the Congressmen who proposed the statehood of Alaska and Hawaii ensured that their bills were introduced, respectively, as S. 49 and H.R. 50.[222] "H.R. 1" is a very desirable title and is usually reserved for highly publicized or anticipated legislation, such as George W. Bush's *No Child Left Behind Act of 2001* (introduced in the 107th Congress).

The Representative or Senator who introduces a bill is known as the bill's *sponsor*. Congressmen are eager to sponsor legislation that will make a favorable impression on their constituents

---

222   Walter J. Oleszek, *Congressional Procedures and the Policy Process*, 4th ed. (Washington, DC: CQ Press, 1996), 97.

back home. Non-controversial bills or those enjoying wide public support often have dozens of co-sponsors. For example, in the 108th Congress, H.R. 1368 proposed that a post office building in Stockton, CA, be named after a former congressman from California. The bill was sponsored by every representative from the state—52 in all. Often, two or more congressmen from opposing parties will co-sponsor a bill in order to demonstrate or encourage bipartisan support.

In Committee

The introduction of a bill is only the first step in the often painstaking process of passing legislation. "Congressional procedures require bills to overcome numerous hurdles. At each stage, measures and procedures must receive majority approval," writes scholar Walter J. Oleszek. "All along the procedural route, therefore, strategically located committees, groups, or individuals can delay, block, or change proposals if they can form majority coalitions. Bargaining may be necessary at each juncture to build the majority coalition that advances the bill to the next step in the legislative process. . . . Inaction or postponement at any stage of the process can mean the defeat of a bill."[223]

After a bill is introduced in the House or Senate, it is assigned to one or more committees for review. Almost all significant legislative activity takes place in these congressional "workshops."[224] Congress has three kinds of committees: standing, select, and joint

---

223   *Ibid.*, 20, 22.
224   Davidson and Oleszek, 193.

committees. *Standing committees* are permanent, having jurisdiction over perennial legislative issues such as education or the armed services. *Select* or *special committees* are established temporarily to investigate a particular issue or controversy. In contrast to standing committees, select committees do not review legislation, but instead conduct special investigations with the purpose of reporting back to Congress. These activities fulfill one of Congress' most important responsibilities, which is the oversight of government activity. The most publicized select committees tend to be those created to investigate possible corruption. Political scandals such as Watergate, Iran-Contra, and Whitewater have all been the subjects of select committee investigations. *Joint committees* consist of members from both houses of Congress. Some joint committees advise the president on a given issue such as taxation, while others oversee congressional services such as the Government Printing Office.

Committee members are appointed by party leaders in each congressional chamber. In each committee, seats are usually divided between Republicans and Democrats, according to each party's holdings in the House and Senate.[225] The beginning of each new Congress is characterized by a competition between newly-elected officials for coveted committee seats. Congressmen vie for committee spots which will enable them to benefit their re-election fundraising and their constituents, sometimes in that order. For example, a Representative whose district includes a military base lobbies for

---

225   The exceptions to this rule are the House Committee on Standards of Official Conduct and the Select Senate Committee on Ethics, both of which have equal party membership.

a spot on the House Armed Services Committee; a Senator from a largely rural state welcomes a seat on the Senate Agriculture, Nutrition and Forestry Committee.

The activity within a committee is controlled by the chairman, who wields a tremendous amount of authority. The chairman decides which bills come up for consideration and how long they should be debated. This power entitles the chair to expedite legislation he or she supports, and to delay legislation he or she opposes. Chairmen often consult with the majority leadership to craft legislative strategies and to work toward party goals.

Once a bill arrives in committee, the chairman has a few options. If he or she disapproves of the bill for any reason, he or she may refrain from adding it to the committee agenda. If the chairman delays the bill in this way until the end of the term, the bill will automatically expire. In fact, a committee may choose to table a bill indefinitely at any time during the review process. This "tabling" power is often used by the chairman or committee members as a bargaining tool, or to suspend legislation from the opposition party. However, if the chairman approves of a bill or believes that it has promise, he or she usually assigns it to a subcommittee. Subcommittees specialize in certain aspects of the committee's jurisdiction. For example, the House Committee on Veterans' Affairs has three subcommittees: Benefits, Health and Oversight and Investigations. Committees with broad jurisdictions, such as the House Appropriations Committee, may have as many as 13 subcommittees.

Once a bill has arrived in a subcommittee, members generally give it a public *hearing*. Hearings give lawmakers an opportunity to learn more about the bill under review, to evaluate the financial implications of the proposal, and to hear public viewpoints on the matter. During hearings, the committee or subcommittee calls in witnesses to testify either in favor of or in opposition to a bill. Witnesses may include staff members from an executive agency, a policy expert, other members of Congress, or even ordinary citizens. Personal testimonies often help to generate publicity for a bill. For example, the hearings before the Senate Judiciary Committee on the *Unborn Victims of Violence Act* (also called "Laci and Conner's Law") featured a female witness whose unborn child had died as a result of domestic violence. The witness personally urged the committee to approve the bill in order to prevent future crimes such as the one perpetrated against her son.[226] Her testimony put a "human face" on the bill, contributing to its popular support as well as to its eventual passage in Congress.[227]

At this stage, if the committee decides to move a bill forward, it may choose to hold a *markup* session. During a markup, the committee reviews a bill line by line to decide if any changes should be made in wording or content. Amendments are usually offered during this stage in the committee process. Once a subcommittee has

---

226   Senate Judiciary Committee, Legislative Hearing on H.R. 1997, the "Unborn Victims of Violence Act of 2003" or "Laci and Conner's Law," 108th Cong., 2nd sess., 2003.
227   Davidson and Oleszek point out that committee hearings are often specifically structured to boost a bill's support: "Hearings … are often orchestrated as a form of political theater where witnesses who put a human face on a public problem tell a story that may generate public momentum for legislation" (214).

completed a markup, the bill is sent back to the full committee. The full committee will often conduct its own markup of the bill before voting on a final draft. When the committee has finished reviewing and amending the bill, it *reports* the bill to Congress with a written recommendation.[228]

Scheduling and Debating a Bill

Once a bill is reported out of committee, it is placed on one of Congress' legislative *calendars*. Congressional calendars schedule different types of bills for different times during a session, helping to regulate the flow of legislative "traffic." In the House, all bills (except those with little or no opposition) are reviewed by the Rules Committee before coming to the floor. The Rules Committee is widely acknowledged as an instrument of the majority and has been called "the handmaiden of the Speaker."[229] Unlike other House committees, the Rules Committee contains a disproportionately large number of majority members, giving the majority party significant power over the legislative schedule. The committee has the power to decide when a bill will appear on the House floor and how much debate will be allowed on it. The committee also grants "rules" regarding what kinds of amendments may be added to a bill. An *open rule* allows members to offer as many amendments as they wish. A

---

228   A committee may recommend that Congress either approve or reject a bill. All House committees are required to submit their reports in writing, and though Senate committees are not held to this requirement, they usually do the same.
229   Porter Goss (R-FL), a former representative, quoted in Oleszek, 137. Goss sat on the Rules Committee under Speaker Newt Gingrich (1995-1999), who used the committee to great advantage.

closed rule usually restricts amendments to those already offered in committee. A *modified rule* allows amendments on certain parts of a bill while prohibiting them on others. Majority members on the Rules Committee often work with majority leaders in the House to expedite the bills they favor or to delay those they oppose. On rare occasions, the President enters the bargaining arena. In 1961, in order to ensure passage of his "New Frontier" legislation, President John F. Kennedy lobbied Speaker Sam Rayburn to enlarge the Democratic majority on the Rules Committee.[230]

In the Senate, decision-making is at times more casual. One congressional expert has said: "If the House is characterized by devotion to rules and parliamentary procedures, the Senate is much more informal, often transacting its business by gentlemen's agreements, with the rules ignored or set aside."[231] In the Senate, schedules and legislative details are often decided on the basis of *unanimous consent* agreements. These agreements are usually negotiated off the floor. On the one hand, unanimous consent agreements are extremely helpful in expediting the legislative process. On the other hand, they are often difficult to obtain. If a single Senator objects to a proposed compromise, for example, he or she can derail an entire agreement. Consequently, Senators are forced to work together closely on an individual, rather than a party, basis. Senator Sam Nunn of Georgia phrased it more colloquially: "Any time you want to legislate around here [in the Senate] you have to convince an awful lot of people over a long period of time to get

---

230   *Ibid.*
231   *Ibid.*, 194.

something accomplished."[232]

When the rules for debate and amendment have been set, the bill is introduced to the floor of the House or Senate. Floor debate offers opponents of the bill unique opportunities for delaying or even killing a bill. One of the most notorious of these tactics is the *filibuster*. Used by the minority to delay legislation, the filibuster is characterized by various time-wasting activities, such as the making of long, drawn-out speeches or offering unnecessary amendments to a bill. Though technically available to members of both houses of Congress, the filibuster is more effective in the Senate, where no time limit can be placed on debate except by unanimous consent. For this reason, a single disgruntled Senator can launch a filibuster. Indeed, even the threat of a filibuster can be enough to force a compromise or concession.

The longest filibuster in Senate history was carried out by Strom Thurmond, D-SC, who held the floor single-handedly for more than 24 hours in opposition to the Civil Rights Act of 1957. The only way to end a filibuster (other than by unanimous consent) is for the Senate to invoke *cloture*. The cloture rule, created in 1917, automatically ends a filibuster upon the vote of three-fifths of the Senate (or 60 of the 100 members). Recently, the rules regarding the filibustering of federal judges and nominees have changed considerably in that only a simple majority is now needed for cloture, although the legislative filibuster is still in place.

A bill is always considered first in the chamber of its

---

232   *Ibid.*, 224.

origin, although all bills dealing with the raising of revenue are to originate in the House.[233] For instance, if a bill is introduced in the House, it must first be reviewed by House committees and debated on and passed by the House before being sent to the Senate for consideration. Once in the Senate, the bill is discussed and amended both in committee and on the floor. At the end of this process, if the Senate passed the bill, it returns the bill and the accompanying changes to the House. If the House and Senate disagree on any part of the bill, they agree to form a *conference committee*. A conference committee consists of members from both chambers who discuss the bill and, if possible, strike a compromise. Upon reaching agreement, the committee sends a draft of the amended bill to both houses of Congress for a re-vote. If approved by both the House and the Senate, the bill is *enrolled*, or a final draft is prepared to be sent to the President.

Presidential Action

Article I, Section 7 of the Constitution states: "Every order, resolution, or vote, to which the concurrence of the senate and house of representatives may be necessary . . . shall be presented to the President of the United States; and before the same shall take effect, shall be approved by him. . . ." When a bill comes before the President, he may take one of several actions. If he approves the bill, he may sign it into law. If he opposes it, he may *veto* it and send it

---

233   On many occasions, sponsors arrange for versions of the same bill to be introduced in both chambers at the same time. The example above is given to high-light the independent (if coordinated) processes that occur in the House and Senate.

back to Congress with his objections. Congress may *override* the President's veto by a two-thirds vote of both houses, upon which the bill becomes law. If the President takes no action at all, the bill automatically becomes law after 10 days, excluding Sundays. Another option is the *pocket veto*, available only near the end of a congressional term. If the President receives a bill less than 10 days (not counting Sundays) before the congressional session ends, he may put the bill aside and let it expire on its own. The unsigned bill cannot be carried over to the next legislative session, and those interested in its passage must start the lawmaking process all over again.

Who Gets the Credit?

The successful passage of a bill, especially one which enjoys broad support, is often marked by several parties jockeying for credit. Who is ultimately responsible for legislation? The President and his administration often claim credit—justifiably—for a popular law. But as we have seen, Congress does much of the hard work required to construct and define that law. So who in Congress gets the credit? Perhaps the leadership, who made sure the bill landed in the right committee. Perhaps the committee chairman, who made sure the bill landed in the right subcommittee. Perhaps the bill's sponsor, without whom the bill might never have come to the attention of Congress. Then again, the bill might never have come to the attention of the sponsor without pressure from special interests. For that matter, no one would be in Congress if not for the American citizens who comprise special interests and who elect their representatives every term. Needless to say, successful legislation can rarely be attributed to only one or two persons or groups. Ultimately, the laws of the United States are produced and maintained by the American people, and thus tend to reflect the character of the people.

CHAPTER FIFTEEN

Judicial Activism and the American Courts

———————◆———————

"The President," wrote de Tocqueville, "can fail without the state's suffering because the President has only a limited duty. Congress can err without the Union's perishing because above Congress resides the electoral body that can change its mind by changing its members. But if the Supreme Court ever came to be composed of imprudent or corrupt men, the confederation would have to fear anarchy or civil war."[234]

De Tocqueville recognized, perhaps even more than some of the Founders, the potential for unrestrained power in the judicial branch. The judiciary itself is essential to the government because it balances the power of the legislature and the executive, and serves as a "depository" of American law. But the misuse of judicial power frustrates the equilibrium of government and endangers the sovereignty of the people. While many Anti-Federalists focused on the lack of a bill of rights during the ratification fights, some, like

---

234   de Tocqueville, 142.

Brutus, the pseudonym of a 1788 Anti-Federalist writer in New York state, would highlight the very real dangers in a Supreme Court that overstepped its bounds: "The judicial power will operate to effect, in the most certain, but yet silent and imperceptible manner. . . an entire subversion of the legislative, executive and judicial powers of the individual states. . . .That the judicial power of the United States, will lean strongly in favor of the general government, and will give such an explanation to the Constitution . . . is very evident from a variety of reasons."[235] Brutus would close out his 11th essay by simply stating: "The power in the judicial, will enable them to mould the government, into almost any shape they please."[236] Brutus's words foretold what would take place in starting in the 19th century until the present day as judicial activism, spearheaded by the Supreme Court and aided by Progressive reform, significantly reshaped American government and society.

Establishment of the Judiciary

The members of the Constitutional Convention left few detailed instructions for the design of the judiciary. In Article III of the Constitution, they simply wrote: "The judicial power of the United States shall be vested in one Supreme Court, and in such inferior courts as the Congress may from time to time ordain and establish." In 1789, the First Congress passed the Judiciary Act,

---

235   *The Debate on the Constitution; Federalist and Antifederalist Speeches, Articles, and Letters During the Struggle over Ratification, Part Two,* (New York, The Library of America, 1993), 133.
236   *Ibid.,* 135.

establishing a network of federal courts consisting of three levels: the district courts, the appellate courts, and the Supreme Court. This system, which has changed little except in size since it was established, handles all criminal or civil cases involving federal law.

The lowest level of the judicial branch consists of 94 district courts spread throughout the country.[237] Most federal cases are resolved at this level. However, if a litigant is unsatisfied with a decision, he or she has the option of appealing his or her case to a court of appeals. The United States has 13 appellate courts, each of which presides over a particular geographic area. When an appellate or circuit court reviews the decision of a lower court, it either affirms or overrules it. As with the district courts, most decisions handed down by courts of appeals are not challenged. But occasionally a litigant will take the final step in the appeals process and petition his case to the United States Supreme Court. While the Supreme Court informally reviews most appeals it receives, it is under no legal obligation (with a few exceptions) to grant any case a formal hearing. Usually, the Court hears only cases that address a pertinent national issue or an unsettled question of constitutional law.

Each state maintains a three-tiered judicial system very similar in design to the national judiciary. Traditionally, the final stop for cases involving state law is the state's Supreme Court. But since the passage of the 14th Amendment (1868) and the establishment of the doctrine of incorporation, the U.S. Supreme Court has assumed the right to review decisions made by state courts.

---

237   Administrative Office of the U.S. Courts, Federal Judiciary, http://www. uscourts.gov (accessed December 15, 2004).

One of the oldest controversies surrounding the Supreme Court is the power of *judicial review*. Judicial review entitles the Court to declare void any federal law that it interprets to be unconstitutional.[238] The doctrine of judicial review was first articulated by Chief Justice John Marshall in *Marbury v. Madison* (1803) when he struck down a section of the Judiciary Act. In his ruling, Marshall wrote: "It is emphatically the province and duty of the judicial department to say what the law is. . . . If then the courts are to regard the Constitution; and the Constitution is superior to any ordinary act of the legislature; the Constitution, and not such ordinary act, must govern the case to which they both apply."[239]

However, implicit in this power to declare the constitutionality of a given law is the power to interpret the Constitution itself. Over time, the way in which Supreme Court justices have chosen to interpret the Constitution has profoundly affected the Court's role both in government and in society. In 1832, Chief Justice John Marshall handed down his decision in *Worcester vs. Georgia* that struck down Georgia laws regarding the ability of white people to come and go on Cherokee lands. President Andrew Jackson, in what was likely an apocryphal statement, commented upon hearing of the ruling, "John Marshall has made his ruling. Now let him enforce it." While likely romanticized, the statement does highlight a central issue with Supreme Court rulings: Congress makes the laws, the Executive signs the laws and then enforces them, but the Judicial

---

238   Since the passage of the Fourteenth Amendment (1868) the Supreme Court has also been able to overturn state law.

239   Marbury v. Madison, 5 U.S. 137 (1803).

is permitted only to rule on the Constitutionality of the laws, not interpret them in such a way as to be the lawgivers. This is the constant tension between the three branches: Who gets to decide what the law *is* and what it *means* and how it is *applied* to society?

Gradual Transformation

When the Founders established the judiciary, they considered it to be the weakest branch of the federal government. In contrast to the Legislative and Executive branches, the Judiciary does not act on its own initiative but only responds to existing lawsuits. It was never meant to be a proactive body, but merely a reactive one. "Whoever attentively considers the different departments of power," wrote Alexander Hamilton, "must perceive, that . . . the judiciary, from the nature of its functions, will always be the least dangerous to the political rights of the Constitution; because it will be least in a capacity to annoy or injure them."[240] Hamilton's assurances proved legitimate for more than 100 years after the Founding. During that time, justices serving on the Supreme Court were governed by two principles: first, that the original intent of the Constitution was the law of the land; second, that a justice's sole responsibility was to guard that law, ensuring that it was applied fully and justly. When faced with difficult cases or legal ambiguities, justices often consulted the rich traditions of English common law and the lessons of America's colonial experience for guidance.

During the 20th century, America experienced significant

---

240   Hamilton, *Federalist 78*, 393.

political and societal developments which gradually lured the courts more and more into the public sphere. The first of these developments was the dramatic growth of the federal government. The many programs and agencies established during FDR's New Deal (1933-1936) required an overwhelming amount of legislation. As the government assumed more control over the economy, education, housing and social welfare, people began taking their objections to court. Soon both state and federal courts were making significant decisions on the precise implementation of government policy.

As the judicial branch assumed an active role in society, interest groups began using the courts to achieve their political goals. Civil rights organizations, for example, found litigation to be an effective strategy for advancing their cause, and sometimes for perfectly good reasons. For example, the black citizens of America. Despite the passage of the 14th Amendment in 1868, blacks had continued to suffer open discrimination, particularly in southern states. Often thwarted in their attempts to change the laws through local and state legislatures, blacks began seeking redress from the courts.[241] During the 1940s and 1950s, the National Association for the Advancement of Colored People (NAACP) funded several successful lawsuits against discriminatory policies and social practices.

However, as the century progressed, environmental lobbyists

---

241   Many Southern legislatures had issued various "regulations" designed to keep blacks both politically and economically disadvantaged. See Harold U. Faulkner, The Quest for Social Justice: 1898-1914, vol. 11 of A History of American Life, ed. Dixon R. Fox and Arthur M. Schlesinger (New York: MacMillan, 1931), 10-13.

and consumer rights groups also began using the courts to promote their interests. Litigation became a popular way of advancing causes that lacked both popular support and congressional sanction. Despite protests from lawmakers that this strategy bypassed the democratic process, the Supreme Court became increasingly receptive to "rights" litigation. Under the leadership of Chief Justice Earl Warren (1953-1969) for example, the Court overturned several laws until it achieved nearly full incorporation of the Bill of Rights under the 14th Amendment, known as *Incorporation*. This took away the states' rights as protected by the 10th Amendment, in which all rights and powers not specifically enumerated to the federal government were to remain with the states.

In recent years, many have come to view the Court as a vehicle for achieving social justice and as a super legislative body. William J. Brennan, Jr., a former justice, has referred to the Court as a benevolent guide, helping Americans to make "right" choices. "[F]rom our beginnings," declared Brennan, "a most important consequence of [our] constitutionally created separation of powers has been the American habit, extraordinary to other democracies, of casting social, economic, philosophical and political questions in the form of lawsuits, in an attempt to secure ultimate resolution by the Supreme Court."[242]

As judges became more open to various types of litigation, they also eased the qualifications for filing lawsuits. Before the 1960s, for example, any citizen wanting to protest a government tax

---

242   Justice William J. Brennan, Jr., *Text and Teaching Symposium* (speech, Georgetown University, Washington, DC, October 12, 1985).

policy or regulation was required to demonstrate "direct injury as the result of [the law's] enforcement."[243] But in 1968, the Warren Court lowered this standard, ruling in *Flast v. Cohen* that any taxpayer could access the courts as long as he demonstrated a "nexus" or link between himself and the objectionable tax policy.[244] Such developments eventually opened the door for class-action lawsuits, in which an individual can sue not only on her own behalf but also for others who suffer her grievance. Increased access to the courts has further encouraged citizens to seek social and personal solutions from the judiciary—not from the slow, and sometimes painful, legislative process.

The most significant factor in the expanding role of the courts has been *judicial activism*. Before the 1950s, the Supreme Court traditionally applied constitutional principles to the needs of society. But by mid-century, the Court had begun construing the Constitution to meet calculated social and political objectives, sometimes for morally good reasons. The case of *Brown v. Board of Education of Topeka* in 1954 marked the beginning of this trend. *Brown*, an anti-segregation lawsuit, arose at a time when the nation was increasingly divided over "separate but equal" racial policies, which required blacks to use separate public facilities to prevent them from associating with whites. For many years, the Supreme Court had avoided making a definitive statement on this controversial issue. In *Plessy v. Ferguson* (1896), the Court had upheld the deep South's

---

243   *Frothingham v. Mellon*, 262 U.S. 447 (1923). Until *Flast v. Cohen* in 1968, *Frothingham* was the controlling case on "standing" in taxpayer lawsuits.
244   *Flast v. Cohen*, 392 U.S. 83, 88 S. Ct. 1942 (1968).

notorious "Jim Crow" laws (laws in the South that enforced racial segregation) simply on the basis that such regulations were "enacted in good faith for the promotion of the public good, and not for the annoyance or oppression of a particular class."[245] However, in the years following *Plessy*, civil rights groups were increasingly successful in using litigation to overcome racially-biased policies. In *Brown*, several black families challenged the segregation within their local school districts. When the case was appealed to the Supreme Court, newly-appointed Chief Justice Warren orchestrated a unanimous ruling in favor of the plaintiff and declared school segregation unconstitutional under the 14th Amendment's "equal protection" clause.

While the *Brown* decision earned notoriety for its statement against segregation, it also provoked intense controversy in its handling of the law. The Court's ruling, which overturned state laws all across the South, was alarmingly deficient in legal reasoning. Warren, who wrote the decision, based the ruling on contemporary sociological studies, suggesting that segregation "generates a feeling of inferiority" in black children and "[affects] their hearts and minds in a way unlikely ever to be undone."[246] Regardless of the truth in such studies, it had never before been the Court's place to consult sources other than the law. Unfortunately, *Brown*'s extra-constitutional flavor lent racists a plausible argument against integration. Most schools refused to desegregate, and the Supreme

---

245 *Plessy v. Ferguson*, 163 U.S. 537, 3 S. Ct. 18 (1896). Homer Plessy, who was one-eighth black, challenged a Louisiana statute enforcing the separate seating of blacks and whites on railroad passenger cars. The Court rejected his argument that the law violated the 14th Amendment's "equal protection" clause.
246 *Brown v. Board of Education*, 347 U.S. 483 (1954).

Court found itself in the position of having to enforce its own ruling. Even so, the Court's mandates had limited influence until Congress passed the Civil Rights Act in 1964.[247]

Though *Brown v. Board of Education of Topeka* had little direct impact on public schools, its ruling had lasting implications for American jurisprudence. Judicial activism became an accepted practice, grounded on the doctrine of the "living Constitution." Proponents of this ideology believe that judges should interpret the Constitution in a way that accommodates the current needs of society. This is yet another turning point away from the Founders' intentions. As people began to see government as the giver of rights, they began to accept the courts as the way to achieve policy outcomes. The Constitution was seen more as a document that reflected peoples' current thinking instead of being based on unchangeable transcendent law that did not change with the times. "What the constitutional fundamentals meant to the wisdom of other times cannot be their measure to the vision of our time," said Justice Brennan. "Similarly, what those fundamentals mean to us, our descendants will learn, cannot be the measure to the vision of their time."[248] After all, activists argue, when the Founders wrote the Constitution, they were unable to predict the changes that would befall America in the future. Thus, each new generation of

---

247 Some critics have argued that *Brown* actually hurt the civil rights movement by indicating that "judicial legislation" was the only way to abolish racism in America. Johnson adds to this argument, saying that, at the time of the decision, some "argued … that race, quickly followed by ethnicity, was displacing citizenship as a badge of identity." See Paul Johnson, *A History of the American People* (New York: HarperPerennial, 1997), 954-955.

248 Brennan, *Text and Teaching Symposium.*

justices must ensure that the Constitution keeps pace with changing times. In the minds of those who advocate a "living Constitution," under proper judicial guardianship, the Constitution will evolve as society evolves. The logical conclusion of the "living Constitution" theory is that nine Supreme Court justices essentially dictate the meaning of the Constitution to the public and in so doing become an unelected, lifetime, super-legislative body. Rather than remaining a practical legal document as the Founders designed it to be, the Constitution becomes instead a symbolic shell into which judges inject meaning. The Constitution is then not a road map, but simply "the lodestar for our aspirations," says Justice Brennan. "Like every text worth reading, it is not crystalline. . . . Its majestic generalities and ennobling pronouncements are both luminous and obscure. This ambiguity of course calls forth interpretation, the interaction of reader and text."[249]

Implicit in this judicial duty of interpretation is the belief that ordinary American citizens lack the expertise to make informed decisions about their laws and communities. The courts, therefore, must guide public opinion, ensuring that the people make healthy choices for themselves. For this reason, the modern Supreme Court has been called the "conscience" of the nation.[250] One Yale professor, for example, has praised the Court for "confronting modern Americans with a moral and political agenda that calls upon them to

---

249   *Ibid.*
250   Anthony Lewis, quoted in Raoul Berger, *Government by Judiciary: The Transformation of the Fourteenth Amendment,* 2nd ed. (Indianapolis: Liberty Fund, 1997), 333

heed the voices of their better selves."[251]

One example of "living Constitution" theory in recent years has been judicial handling of the First Amendment. The amendment, which states, "Congress shall make no law respecting an establishment of religion, or prohibiting the free exercise thereof," was originally intended to prevent the federal government from establishing a state church or legally sanctioning a particular religious belief to the detriment of others. This interpretation was more or less observed until the mid-20th century, when judges became more active in the political process. Today, the First Amendment is popularly held to entitle the government to prevent religious belief or practice from influencing public life. In *Lemon v. Kurtzman* (1971), for example, the Supreme Court established a three-part "test" to determine whether or not a specific government action was in violation of the First Amendment. In order to pass the Lemon test, a given law 1) "must have a secular legislative purpose;" 2) "its principal or primary effect must be one that neither advances nor inhibits religion;" and 3) "must not foster 'an excessive entanglement with religion.'"[252]

In recent years, some judges have begun calling for a return to "original intent"—that is, interpreting the Constitution according to what the Founders intended it to mean. Former Attorney General Edwin Meese III has encouraged the courts to "judge policies in the light of principles, rather than remold principles in light of

---

251 Bruce Ackerman, quoted in *ibid.*
252 *Lemon v. Kurtzman*, 403 U.S. 602 (1971).

policies."[253] He warned against "pouring new meaning into old words, [thereby] creating new powers and new rights totally at odds with the logic of our Constitution and its commitment to the rule of law."[254] The Founders, indeed, could not foresee many of the issues Americans face today, but the principles they articulated in the Constitution are timeless and relevant to every generation because of their understanding of human nature and of the dangers of concentrated power.

The question with "living Constitution" judges is if they step beyond such boundaries even to do good, what will prevent them from also doing evil? Only when the courts practice restraint and operate within their prescribed original Constitutional limits will the law rule over man. "[L]aw, without equity," wrote Sir William Blackstone, "though hard and disagreeable, is much more desirable for the public good, than equity without law; which would make every judge a legislator, and introduce most infinite confusion."[255]

253   Edwin Meese III, *American Bar Association* (speech, Washington, DC, July 9, 1985).
254   *Ibid.*
255   William Blackstone, quoted in Johnson, 951.

CHAPTER SIXTEEN
Civic Involvement: Our Republic and You

———————◆———————

In the 2016 Presidential election, turnout among registered voters was at 55%, which was nearly 10 points lower than in the 2008 election. If one were to compare the turnout rates of national elections to off-year state and local elections and primaries, in which turnout rates can be as low as 20 or 30%, the 2016 Presidential results don't seem that paltry. But look at these figures another way. If 55% of registered voters, or almost three out of every five, show up at the polls, that means two out of every five voters stayed home. Should Americans be concerned when 40-45% of their fellow registered voters do not feel it is important to participate in the selection of their most influential leader? Add to this the fact that the number of registered voters reflects little more than half the number of citizens of voting age—meaning that almost 100 million eligible voters are not even registered.

Irish politician John Philpot Curran (1750-1817) once said, "The condition upon which God hath given liberty to man is

eternal vigilance; which condition if he break, servitude is at once
the consequence of his crime and the punishment of his guilt."[256]
Edmund Burke put the same thought another way when he said,
"The only thing necessary for evil to triumph is for good men to do
nothing."[257] On these reflections, one could scarcely conclude that
American democracy is robust and fully healthy. Nevertheless, the
apathy displayed by so many Americans presents an open field of
opportunity for those men and women of virtue and goodwill.

    The Golden Rule cited in the Bible commands Christians
to love our neighbors as we love ourselves. One way we can love our
neighbors in a democratic constitutional republic such as the United
States is to make responsible use of our political rights. It may seem
odd to think of "love" in such political terms, but casting a vote for a
statesman, lobbying your state legislature to repeal an onerous law, or
speaking out against corruption at a local town hall meeting can all
be ways to demonstrate love to your neighbor because it shows that
you actually care. Concepts such as liberty, equality, self-government,
the rule of law, and property rights all bring with them blessings for
all involved. To the degree we use our individual rights to help secure
those broader concepts, we are in fact blessing our neighbors, our
state, our nation. One need not be a U.S. Senator or a Supreme Court
Justice to have a meaningful, positive influence on civic life in America.
But what is required of every American citizen is to fulfill his or her
civic duty by being involved as a good steward of the republic.

---

256   *"Speech upon the Right of Election of the Lord Mayor of Dublin,"* July
10, 1790.
257   Attributed.

Local Politics

"All politics is local." Former Speaker of the U.S. House of Representatives, Thomas "Tip" O'Neill would often invoke this adage to remind his colleagues in Congress that, in the end, people care most about those issues that touch them directly. Some may take an interest in famine relief in Ethiopia or in South American trade policy, however most people will be more concerned about that dangerous intersection or pot hole down the street or an unemployed family member's inability to find substantial work. O'Neill, a liberal Democrat, spent 33 years in the House of Representatives—from 1953 to 1986. Though no one would consider him a champion of conservatism in Congress, he understood a basic truth about politics in a democratic society: To be successful, you must show people how their interests are tied to your policies.

De Tocqueville examined this same concept, localism, from another perspective. He explained that attention to local politics was *necessary* for a free people to maintain their liberty. He wrote, "It is . . . in the township [de Tocqueville's term for local government] that the force of a free people resides. The institutions of a township are to freedom what primary schools are to science; they put it within reach of the people; they make them taste its peaceful employ and habituate them to making use of it. Without the institutions of a township a nation can give itself a free government, but it does not have the spirit of freedom."[258]

That is to say, when we take responsibility for our own local

---

258   de Tocqueville, 57-58.

affairs, we are learning to make effective use of our liberty. We learn the art of self-government. De Tocqueville rightly asserted that free men, well-versed in the art and practice of self-government, become a formidable obstacle to the rise of tyranny. Tyranny thrives when free individuals surrender their local responsibilities and natural rights to a centralized government, often for the sake of mere convenience. Tyranny falters when those same free individuals, acting in concert with like-minded fellow citizens, take responsibility to solve local problems locally.

In most American communities today, the opportunities for local involvement are numerous. Local governing bodies, school boards, town councils and county commissions tend to be very accessible. Most meetings are open to the public and are located close to home rather than at some marble building hundreds or even thousands of miles distant. Many important issues such as large purchases, building projects, zoning changes and tax adjustments must first be the subject of a *public hearing*, the purpose being to gather community input. Because local elections tend to be decided by comparatively small numbers of votes, local officials also tend to be responsive to reasonable concerns of residents. Indeed, many local "problems" can be resolved with modest effort by attentive and organized citizens.

Organizing at the local level need not be daunting. Neighbors tend to have common interests, but lack knowledge of impending issues. What is often needed is a prime mover, a catalyst— someone who can galvanize the community around common interests. Active community leaders can inform their neighbors and organize effective countermeasures. Outcomes at the local level are frequently determined simply by those who bother to "show up," and even when showing up is not enough, determination and diligence are typically the best predictors of success.

Local election campaigns present another excellent opportunity for the civically minded. Whether the motivation is to turn out an unfit office-holder or simply to provide a more positive influence in government, local elections can be a legitimate and important focus of the civic-minded citizen. While national elections tend to generate more excitement, local election campaigns chronically suffer from a lack of interest. Consequently, an energetic volunteer on a local campaign can often gain more hands-on experience than he or she would on a well-funded, well-staffed national campaign. Furthermore, local parties often have difficulty recruiting candidates for what are perceived to be "lesser" offices. Under such circumstances, even young and inexperienced candidates can win elections through sheer effort. To win a Congressional election one must usually secure tens of thousands of votes, less than a thousand votes can achieve victory at the local level. And, of course, these sorts of experiences gained at the local level can be useful for those who do move on to larger campaigns.

If one is looking for an even greater example of success at the local level, and the changes that can be made, it should be pointed out that the Progressive movement at the turn of the 20th century did not begin at the top, in Washington, DC. It began as a state and local reform movement, building from the ground up. It was a response to corruption, albeit with wrong solutions, that over the course of 25 years fundamentally changed American government through the birthing of the Administrative State, by removing some of the constitutional machinery, but just as importantly, changing the mindset of many Americans and how they perceived government and its role. From that roughly one generation in time, our constitutional republic changed dramatically, and because of it, so did our society.

State Politics

As we have seen, state sovereignty was an important concept for the American Founders. The Constitution as written, and originally understood, envisioned a federal system of two separate spheres of power, one superintended by the national government, the other superintended by the states; in short, the concept of federalism. Each was to be sovereign in its own sphere and create a tension between the two that protected Americans' rights and prevented the national government from becoming too strong.

However, a series of events as previously noted above and attitudinal changes have altered the intended relationship between the state governments and the national government. If anything like federalism is to be reestablished in contemporary America, structural changes like the repeal of the 17th Amendment must happen, but it also means that responsible citizens will have to invest more time and attention in their state governments.

Like local politics, state politics are usually viewed as less glamorous and less important than national politics. Yet, even the residual of power held by state governments today influences our lives in substantial ways. Education, criminal law, and transportation, though certainly influenced by the national government, remain substantially state issues. Some of the most effective pro-life laws— for example, "heart-beat" bills, parental notification, informed consent, and 24-hour waiting period laws—have come from state governments, not the national government. State government affects our lives on a daily basis through sales taxes, property taxes and income taxes. To abandon state government to unrepresentative forces is unacceptable. On the contrary, except for a very limited number of liberal states on the coasts, conservatives can dominate the overwhelming majority of the remaining states if they are willing to put forth the effort.

At the state level, the premium on concerted effort is even greater than at the local level. While a single voice can sometimes move local officials to action, such is far more unlikely among state legislators and governors. One good way to influence state politics is by supplying information and labor. Many state legislators are part-time, meaning their time is limited. Unlike U.S. Congressmen who have extensive staff budgets and numerous paid, professional aides, state legislators have little or no staffing resources to facilitate legal research and the like. Because of this, many state legislators are more than willing to accept the volunteer assistance of civically active citizens. Individuals willing to do the leg-work of the legislative process without compensation can be very influential in the outcome.

Here again, opportunities for involvement in election campaigns are numerous. While money is a more important campaign need at the state level than at the local level, most state legislative districts are still small enough that labor-intensive *grassroots* campaign techniques can be effective, even in the absence of expensive television and radio ads. These grassroots techniques include door-to-door knocking and live conversations, local meet-and-greet forums, and various other forms of direct vote solicitation. Even in our high-tech age, there is no substitute for direct, personal, informed appeals between neighbors. What state campaigns often lack, however, is the extensive manpower that grassroots campaigning requires. Too often, good candidates, capable of serving their states well, fail to gain office simply for lack of sufficient campaign help.

National Politics

For most people, when they think of politics, they think of politics at the national level. The word "election" conjures up images of presidential candidates in navy blue suits wearing red ties squaring off in debates or delivering a rousing speech to enthusiastic state delegations at a national party convention. For reasons we have already covered, state and local politics can be *the* vital battleground in the fight to restore America. Still, there is no denying that many of the decisive issues of our time are the prerogative of the national government.

The federal government is in disarray and has been getting worse for some time. One may ask why more conservatives, especially in the evangelical community, did not step up sooner. The answer is found in the Christian fundamentalist movement of the early 20th century. Early fundamentalism taught that politics was a worldly pursuit, unworthy of a true Christian. The events surrounding the infamous Scopes Trial of 1925 seemed to confirm that true faith and the public square did not mix. As a result, many evangelicals withdrew from politics, as well as from other fields thought to be too worldly. In the decades that followed, American law and politics began to show the effects of evangelical abdication. In the public debates surrounding the Vietnam War and Watergate, for example, conservative Christian voices were largely silent. We should not, however, forget that the Catholic Church and Roman Catholics remained present and engaged on the abortion and life issue. It is because of their determination not to abandon the issue, and the foundation they laid, that we have seen many of the victories in recent years on the life issue.

Unfortunately, with the fundamentalist retreat into separation came a moral decline in American culture. New problems began to agitate the country, including abortion, euthanasia, and the gay agenda. In the late 1970s, a new generation of fundamentalists and conservative Christians began to take note. A major turning point was the creation of the Moral Majority, a Christian conservative grassroots organization dedicated to restoring a Christian influence in politics. Founded by the Reverend Jerry

Falwell and others, the Moral Majority called evangelicals back to the polls to stem the tide of cultural forces they deemed destructive. The election of Ronald Reagan to the Presidency in 1980, who praised this movement, gave some hope that the trends could be reversed. Reagan's success, however, was not replicated in other branches of government, and by the end of the 1980s there was reason to doubt whether a truly "moral" majority existed in America.

Politically active Christians retooled, and organizations such as the Christian Coalition and the Home School Legal Defense Association came to the fore. Such organizations understood that they were in competition with liberal, secular cultural elites (in the media, Hollywood, the music industry, etc.) for the hearts of Middle America. Rather than simply calling a real or imagined majority to the polls, they argued for the prudence of their positions and formed broad coalitions of like-minded believers of various stripes.

The outcome is still in the balance. If concerted effort is important at the state level, it is absolutely critical at the national level. One does not steer the ship of a state 330 million people strong all alone. One must have allies. Today, a number of large religious conservative organizations contend with liberal and secular opponents at the national level over specific issues (such as National Right to Life) and public policy in general (Concerned Women for America, the Family Research Council, as well as others already mentioned). These cooperative organizations represent opportunities for civically-minded Christians to influence national politics. Another way to influence national politics is to help elect the best statesmen to national office. A Congressional campaign is an extensive operation. A Presidential campaign is larger still.

Ultimately, a better national government will require better candidates. But unless one rises to prominence in some unconventional fashion—sometimes a sports star or military hero or a wealthy real estate developer and TV star can be immediately successful in national politics—running for Congress or higher office is usually the result of many years of more humble service. It takes time to build a truly successful national movement; even the Progressives took decades to enact change, but that took place only after years of organizing and agitating at the state and local level.

Those who seek to bring about fundamental national generational change must disabuse themselves of the notion that somehow, after decades of wrong trends and decisions, that magically overnight all will be made well with a silver bullet. This is naive, but it is also destructive, because it removes the idea that it will take consistent hard work, over the course of years, to bring about the necessary change.

CHAPTER SEVENTEEN
Who Will We Be as a People?

---◆---

Today we find ourselves 232 years removed from the final ratification of the Constitution, in a world that our Founders could not have imagined: from the combustion engine to space and jet travel to the internet and a world with mass automation and artificial intelligence. We've made great progress as a people, exorcising the demon of slavery, acknowledging in a real way that all men and women, regardless of race, are equal. Along the way, we've become the longest lasting constitutional republic in history.

We were given a great gift, one that we take for granted far too often: as We the People, the very foundation of our constitutional republic, we've experienced a degree of prosperity and power and freedom that great empires of the past couldn't even begin to fathom. As a self-governing people, we are stewards and guardians of this great nation, not only for our own freedoms, but for the freedom of our children and our children's children.

However, we have many challenges before us: Many pieces

of the machinery of the republic, put in place to protect our rights, have been knocked down and removed. We find that many of our leaders have lost sight of their chief purpose: to protect the rights and promote the interests of the American people, the American taxpayer. It is immoral to do otherwise, and yet leadership in both major parties continue on with their immoral behavior, prioritizing other interests above the American people.

The great question we must ask ourselves as Americans is, "Where do we go from here?" As we stand here in the 21st century, we must decide who we are as a people, what these forms of the Constitution and the Bill of Rights actually mean, and what do we truly want. But more importantly, we must ask, "Who are the people who make a constitutional republic work?"

There used to be a common set of beliefs about human nature, the role of government, and transcendent truths. That framework of beliefs was the foundation upon which our government was built. It is obvious, but it must be clearly stated so there are no misunderstandings: This constitutional republic, our system of government, codified in the Constitution and Bill of Rights, simply institutionalized what people already believed. And the beliefs encapsulated in those documents were from a Judeo-Christian, Anglo-American belief system.

The Constitution isn't some magically self-perpetuating document. It persists because of the people's belief systems behind the document and the actions they take to live accordingly, then and now. But at the end of the day, the Constitution is a piece of paper that codifies beliefs and frames out how a government is to operate based on those understood beliefs. As John Francis Mercer, a delegate from Maryland to the Constitutional Convention, wrote, "It is a great mistake to suppose that the paper we are to propose will govern the United States. It is the men whom it will bring into the Government and interest in maintaining it that is to govern them. The paper will only mark out the mode and the form. Men are the substance and must do the business."[259] So what are the views of those people? What are the beliefs, values, morals, principles of those people that truly give life to a robust and healthy republic? What do they believe and how do they live out those beliefs?

The men and women who initially came to these shores in the 17th century were primarily middle to upper middle class, or quickly became so upon arriving on these shores. They were a self-sufficient, risk-taking, non-conformist, and individualistic people who self-selected and voluntarily associated, who boarded small wooden ships and sailed for months across the thousands of miles of the Atlantic Ocean to a new world. In hindsight, is it really so hard to see where the American entrepreneurial, individualist, and non-conformist character came from?

These people who came were primarily a religious people, and even those who were not religious still moved within the framework of a Judeo-Christian worldview. These beliefs, or value set, informed how they viewed the world around them and how they responded to it. As historian Clinton Rossiter wrote, "It must never

---

259   *Madison's Notes to the Debates in the Federal Convention of 1787*, 14 August 1787.

be forgotten, especially in an age of upheaval and disillusionment, that American democracy rests squarely on the assumption of a pious, honest, self-disciplined, moral people. For all its faults and falterings, for all the distance it has yet to travel, American democracy has been and remains a highly moral adventure."[260] To say that we've drifted away from this understanding is a mild understatement.

We've lost common values, common views. We can no longer define words the same way; we might use the same terms, but our definitions vary. This is not a mistake: The Left knows that whoever wins the debate on how we define words and frames how we actually debate a topic typically wins the battle for a culture and civilization. The Left has decided that there really aren't transcendent truths—and that is a highly irrational declaration. We can defy higher moral law, we can deny transcendent truths, but we cannot alter them. They still exist outside of us and our passing whims.

Some have decided these laws and truths are inconvenient and have decided that they prefer a moral relativism that changes with the times to reflect whatever society deems acceptable. What we are left with then, since there is no higher law, no absolute truth, is simply competing opinions as one side feels that what they believe is right, and the other believes the opposite. One rages against the other about not being factual, not being truthful, while ignoring the absurdity of it all: Whose truth? Whose facts? This is all very problematic for a society. As philosopher Francis Schaeffer once

---

260 Clinton Rossiter, *Seedtime of the Republic; The Origin of the American Tradition of Political Liberty* (New York; Harcourt, Brace and Company, 1953), 55.

wrote, human nature desires peace and prosperity. It cannot and will not tolerate a tension and strife in society. Therefore if there is no transcendent truth, there must be a politically manufactured truth, a *facilitated* truth, in which one side must win out and compel the other side to accept its opinions as "truth." Sadly the only way resolution is reached in these situations is by might, by force.

We have allowed this to take place because moral relativism and identity politics have taken hold and brought about a fracturing and Balkanization of society. Not only does it turn our motto, *E pluribus unum*, on its head by essentially saying, "Out of one, many," it gives credence to a variety of beliefs and "moral value" systems in which all are considered equally and morally on the same plane.

So what do we believe about human nature right now? Human nature has always been a struggle between the savage and the divine, between what we "can do" versus what "we should do" in which our imperfect human nature struggles to follow a higher calling. We must accept that we are imperfect: We're no angels. While we are capable of great good, we are incapable of sustained good. Nothing will work unless we accept that truth. It is in the acceptance of real human nature that we can then be realistic about the challenges we confront.

The morality of a government is really just the reflection of individual morality. When we say that decline is a choice, it's the choices of the individual and what he or she chooses to accept, that leads to decline. These choices are intentional. Thus the belief in individual responsibility and self-governance, for a healthy self-governing republic is built upon and is a reflection of a society of self-governing people. But the self-governance grows out of a moral system, for why govern oneself unless there is a belief in right and wrong and actual consequences and rewards, both temporal and eternal, for those actions. The Founders had very specific ideas on the moral framework that provided and gave order and a basis for self-governance: "The men of 1776 believed that the good state would rise on the rock of private and public morality, that morality was in the case of most men and all states the product of religion, and that the earthly mission of religion was to set men free."[261]

So we must ask ourselves again what we truly believe because it is only a people with a firm moral belief and resolve that will be able to navigate what confronts us, from mass automation and the period of transition and potential upheaval that will bring, to illegal immigration and aggressive proponents of infanticide to external challenges from authoritarian police states and the internal siren songs of socialism. Only a people who know what they believe and have the proper framework for making decisions will be able to meet these challenges head on and triumph.

We Choose Not to Decline: We Choose to Be Great

America's greatest days do not have to be behind her: They can be in front of her if we make the right choices. The question is whether the American people and her leaders have the courage to do so. We must first reaffirm our belief that every individual

---

261   Rossiter, 59

human being, born and unborn, has been given natural rights that no man or government can take away. We must view government not as the giver of rights or as a provider, but the guardian of the rights of its citizens, and that those citizens, by coming together into just and voluntary association, choose to charge their duly elected representatives, and the government they formed, with being the stewards of those rights.

But we cannot simply declare these ideas: These ideas and beliefs must inspire intentional action. Action is the soul of revolution and we must have a revolution in our thinking and approach to government. If we truly believe that government must be limited in size and scope, we must be willing to shut down departments and agencies and devolve power out of Washington DC. Today we have a massive administrative state of more than 430 departments, agencies and sub-agencies; we must intentionally shrink this number. An audit of those various departments and agencies would no doubt show a significant number of redundancies.

There are a number of other actions that we could take. We could shut down the Department of Energy and retain only the essential functions and place them into the Departments of Defense, Interior, and Commerce. We should shut down the Progressives' golden calf of the Consumer Financial Protection Bureau: It is a bureau of 1,600 employees that is outside of Congressional oversight and serves only to truly protect and advance the interests of the Progressive left. Furthermore, as the Trump Administration has already begun doing with the Department of Agriculture, in proposing to move it out of DC, in the process of shrinking government, we should also break apart the leviathan and place it in different parts of the country. Not only does this devolve power out of DC, it places what is a dangerously detached government closer to the people it serves, which has been one of the great problems we've seen develop over the last century. We must also consider migrating the roughly 800,000 non-essential federal government employees into the private sector, which currently is replete with job openings, eradicating those non-essential positions from the federal rolls.

We must also seriously consider reinstating some of the machinery of our republic, specifically repealing the 17th Amendment. That repeal would return states once more to the important place they deserve at the table in Washington, DC. It would return the U.S. Senate once more to being the States' House, making Senators once more truly representatives of their states' interests and not the little kings many perceive themselves to be. By returning the appointment of Senators to the state legislators, we would once again emphasize the importance of state elections and the need for even greater civic engagement.

We must also be willing to say that there are no institutions or individuals who are too big to fail. If we truly believe in the rule of law and the equal application of law, then every individual, regardless of last name or power or money, must stand equal before it and bear the consequences for his or her actions. If we believe that the law is king, and not the king is law, we must determine to act in such a way that is consistent with that belief. To have a bifurcated legal system that protects the interests of the powerful and neglects the interests of the average citizen is to sow the seeds of our demise. We must also believe and accept that there are no institutions such as the Department of Justice or the FBI that are above the Constitution and the Bill of Rights. The American public needs to understand, regardless of left or right, that from now on, there is protection for all views and thoughts and speech if we will return to this idea of rule of law.

We must reform higher education and healthcare by demanding greater transparency. Is it really too much to ask that those industries, given incredible benefits via the tax regulations governing non-profits offering services, should be required to have absolute pricing transparency and unleash true market forces which lead to consumer-centric industries?

We must also confront the various technology and social media companies, break apart monopolies and redefine them correctly for what they are: publishers and telecommunications companies. In dealing with these companies, we must advance the idea of data sovereignty, that as with all property rights, both physical and intellectual, personal data is the individual's natural right.

As artificial intelligence increasingly plays a role in our society and will eventually become a part of our individual and daily lives, our leaders show little appreciation for how mass automation is being accelerated by the abuse of personally identifiable data. They also appear either ignorant or disinterested in how that automation will displace many American workers. This nation is headed into a great transition period, perhaps lasting 30 to 40 years, as automation displaces more and more workers. In response to this transition, there must be solutions. How will we handle this transition period and provide opportunities for the American worker to make a living and evolve into the new reality? Perhaps in that transition period one such solution would be responsible energy exploration on federal lands which could lead to a multi-trillion-dollar massive infrastructure fund based on royalties. Out of this would arise a new Great Works program that would allow workers to make a living wage, revitalizing American roads and bridges and cities while not adding any new taxes for the American people. It could also lead to welfare reform, lessening Americans' tax burdens for the social welfare systems while applying John Smith's famous adage from Jamestown: *If you do not work, you shall not eat.* All able-bodied people currently on welfare rolls could be put to work.

In the face of illegal immigration, mass automation, and an already significant tax burden to fund welfare systems, our leaders must confront the madness and insanity of importing, every month, "small cities" of low-skilled and unskilled workers into this country. The solution most assuredly involves securing, with physical barriers, our southern border and replacing our current immigration system of reunification, chain migration and anchor babies into one that is merit based.

With a call to greater civic engagement to preserve and advance our republic, it would be beneficial for the American people that Election Day were made a national holiday and a celebration of all the traditions that have made our republic great. While ensuring the sanctity of the individual vote with reforms such as photo identification, in-person, on Election Day (except in extreme circumstances such as military deployment or disabled individuals), using paper ballots, the national Election Day holiday would emphasize civics and patriotism and love of country.

Keep America Free

If you were to take the entirety of the Founders' writings, from their correspondence to their deliberations, their public documents and debates and compress the essence of all of that into a few simple words, it would be these: **Keep America Free**. Every motivation and action would be toward that goal: To keep the American people as free as possible, both from domestic governmental intrusion and also from foreign domination. That domestic freedom allowed Americans to thrive as a people and economically, and those intentional decisions allowed America the economic strength to respond to threats to global freedom multiple times in the 20th century.

The question remains for us today: Will we choose to keep America free? Dr. Joseph Warren, addressing the people of Boston in 1772, in the face of the oppression of the British Crown and Parliament, expressed his hopes for America: "May we ever be a people favoured of God. May our land be a land of liberty, the seat of virtue, the asylum of the oppressed, a name and a praise in the whole earth." While imperfect, since our Founding, we have sought to be that beacon of hope for all freedom-loving people. We now have a duty and an obligation, not only to those who will follow us, but to those who came before us. We have been given a great legacy, yet what will we do with it? Ultimately, if decline is a choice, our response must be that we choose not to decline. We choose to be great. We must choose and resolve to be the stewards of the republic our Founding Fathers gave us. Paraphrasing Franklin: *This is our republic, if we choose to keep it.*

ACKNOWLEDGMENTS

A book is never fully the work of a single person and the same is true for this one. Some portions of this book are updated and edited materials previously printed by American Majority over the years. But the final manuscript of *Restoring Our Republic* would never have come to fruition were it not for my good friend, Paul Bonicelli, PhD. Numerous weekends were spent reading, expanding, editing, and refining the book. His time and insights were invaluable. My mother, Anne Ryun, played a role as well in editing the book, as did a friend from many years ago who I reconnected with over this project: Carol Blair, who edited the book. My sister-in-law, Rachel Parker who typeset and designed the book, gave the book its look and feel, for which I'm very grateful. For Raheem Kassam who gave me great insights in bringing this book to the public. And to my wife, Becca, for supporting me through the entire process.

WORKS CONSULTED

Barker, Ernest, ed. and trans. *The Politics of Aristotle*. London: Oxford University Press, 1946.

Bailyn, Bernard ed., *The Debate on the Constitution; Federalist and Antifederalist Speeches, Articles, and Letters During the Struggle over Ratification (Part Two)*. New York City: Library of America, 1993.

Beloff, Max, ed. *The Debate on the American Revolution: 1761-1783*, 2nd ed. London: Adam & Charles Black, 1960.

Bennett, William J. *Our Sacred Honor: Words of Advice from the Founders in Stories, Letters, Poems, and Speeches*. New York: Simon & Schuster, 1997.

Bercovitch, Sacvan. *The American Jeremiad*. Madison, WI: University of Wisconsin Press, 1978.

Berger, Raoul. *Government by Judiciary: The Transformation of the Fourteenth Amendment*, 2nd ed.

Indianapolis: Liberty Fund, 1997.

Bloom, Allan, ed. and trans. *The Republic of Plato*, 2nd ed.

Boorstin, Daniel J. *Americans: The Colonial Experience*. New

York: Vintage Books, 1958.

Bowen, Catherine Drinker. *John Adams and the American*

Revolution. Boston: Little, Brown &

Company, 1950.

--------------. *Miracle at Philadelphia: The Story of the*

Constitutional Convention, May to September 1787. Boston: Little,

Brown & Company, 1966.

Bradford, William. *Of Plymouth Plantation: Bradford's History of*

the Plymouth Settlement, 1608-1650 (Enhanced Media Publishing,

2018

Brown v. Board of Education of Topeka, 347 U.S. 483 (1954).

Bunker, Nick. *Making Haste from Babylon: The Mayflower*

Pilgrims and Their World. New York: Vintage Books, 2010.

Ceaser, James W., ed. *American Government: Origins, Institutions*

and Public Policy, 5th ed. Dubuque, IA: Kendall/Hunt, 1998.

Ceaser, James W. and Andrew E. Busch. *The Perfect Tie: The True*

Story of the 2000 Presidential Election. Lanham, MD: Rowman and & Littlefield, 2001.

Cohen, Jeffrey E. *Politics and Economic Policy in the United States*, 2nd ed. Boston: Houghton Mifflin, 2000.

Davidson, Roger H. and Walter J. Oleszek. *Congress and Its Members*, 9th ed. Washington, DC: CQ Press, 2004.

Dershowitz, Alan M. *America on Trial: Inside the Legal Battles that Transformed Our Nation*. New York: Warner Books, 2004.

Doherty, Brian. *Radicals for Capitalism: A Freewheeling History of the Modern American Libertarian Movement* (New York City: Public Affairs, 2007)

Dolbeare, Kenneth M. *American Political Thought*, 4th ed. Chatham, NJ: Chatham House Publishers, 1998.

Donovan, Frank, ed. *The George Washington Papers*. New York: Dodd, Mead & Co., 1964.

Evans, M. Stanton. *The Theme is Freedom: Religion, Politics, and the American Tradition*. Washington, DC: Regnery, 1994.

Farris, Michael. *Constitutional Law for Christian Students: Original Documents and Decisions of the United States Supreme Court*. Paeonian Springs, VA: Homeschool Legal Defense

Association, 1991.

Faulkner, Harold U. *The Quest for Social Justice: 1898-1914*, vol. 11 of *A History of American Life*, ed. Dixon R. Fox and Arthur M. Schlesinger. New York: MacMillan, 1931.

Flast v. Cohen, 392 U.S. 83, 88 S. Ct. 1942 (1968).

Foner, Eric and Olivia Mahoney. *America's Reconstruction: People and Politics after the Civil War*. Baton Rouge: Louisiana State University Press, 1995.

Frothingham v. Mellon, 262 U.S. 447 (1923).

Gitlow v. People of the State of New York, 268 U.S. 652 (1925).

Griswold v. Connecticut, 391 U.S. 86 S. Ct. 1678 (1965).

Hall, Kermit L., Ed. *The Oxford Companion to the Supreme Court of the United States*. New York: Oxford University Press, 1992.

Hamilton, Alexander, John Jay and James Madison. *The Federalist Papers*, ed. Garry Wills. New York: Bantam Books, 1982.

Hamilton, Alexander, John Jay and James Madison. *The Federalist*, ed. George W. Carey and James McClellan. Indianapolis: Liberty Fund, 2001.

Johnson, Paul. *A History of the American People*. New York: HarperPerennial, 1997.

Johnson, Thomas J., ed. *The Oxford Companion to American History*. New York: Oxford University Press, 1966.

Jost, Kenneth. "Campaign Finance Showdown." The CQ Researcher Online 12, no. 41 (November 22, 2002): 969-992. http://library.cqpress.com/cqresearcher/ cqresrre2002112200 (accessed February 17, 2005).

Kenyon, J.P. *Stuart England*, 2nd ed. London: Penguin, 1978.

Ketcham, Ralph, ed. *The Anti-Federalist Papers and the Constitutional Convention Debates*. New York: Mentor, 1986.

Kirk, Russell. *The American Cause*. Chicago: Henry Regnery Company, 1957.

--------------. *The Portable Conservative Reader*. New York: Viking Penguin, 1982.

--------------. *Rights and Duties: Reflections on Our Conservative Constitution*. Dallas: Spence Publishing, 1997.

--------------. *The Roots of American Order*. La Salle, IL: Open Court, 1974.

Kramnick, Isaac, ed. *The Portable Edmund Burke*. New York: Viking Penguin, 1999.

Literary Classics of the United States. *Benjamin Franklin:*

Writings. New York: Library of America, 1987.

Locke, John. *Two Treatises of Government*, ed. Peter Laslett. New York: Cambridge University, 1960.

Maisel, L. Sandy. *Parties and Elections in America: The Electoral Process*, 2nd ed. New York: McGraw-Hill, 1993.

Marbury v. Madison. 5 U.S. 137 (1803).

Miller, Perry. *Errand into the Wilderness*. Cambridge, MA: Belknap Press and Harvard University, 1956.

Morison, Samuel Eliot. *The Oxford History of the American People*. New York: Oxford University Press, 1965.

Morris, Richard B., ed. *Alexander Hamilton and the Founding of the Nation*. New York: Dial Press, 1957.

O'Brien, David M. *Constitutional Law and Politics*, vol. 2, *Civil Rights and Civil Liberties*, 4th ed. New York: W. W. Norton & Co., 2000.

Oleszek, Walter J. *Congressional Procedures and the Policy Process*, 4th ed. Washington, DC: CQ Press, 1996.

Patrick, John J. *The Bill of Rights; A History in Documents*. New York: Oxford University Press, 2003.

Plessy v. Ferguson, 163 U.S. 537, 3 S. Ct. 18 (1896).

Plutarch. *Pericles*, trans. John Dryden. The Internet Classics Archive, 1994. http://classics.mit.edu/Plutarch/pericles.html.

Pound, Roscoe. Introduction to *American Liberty and 'Natural Law'*, by Eugene Gerhart. Boston: Beacon Press, 1953.

Prettyman, E. Barrett, Jr. "Thoughts on Justice Jackson's Unpublished Opinion of *Brown v. Board of Education*." Speech given at the Athenaeum Hotel, Chautauqua, NY, October 8, 2003.

Renstrom, Peter G. *Constitutional Rights Sourcebook*. Santa Barbara: ABC-CLIO, 1999.

Richard, Carl J. *The Founders and the Classics: Greece, Rome, and the American Enlightenment*. Cambridge: Harvard University Press, 1994.

Rossiter, Clinton. *Seedtime of the Republic; The Origin of the American Tradition of Political Liberty*. New York; Harcourt, Brace and Company, 1953.

Salem Press. *U.S. Court Cases: Law and the Courts*. 2 vols. Pasadena, CA: Salem Press, 1999.

Schlesinger, Jr., Arthur M., ed. *The Almanac of American History*. New York: G.P. Putnam's Sons, 1983.

Skousen, W. Cleon. *The Making of America; The Substance and Meaning of the Constitution.* Washington, DC: The National Center for Constitutional Studies, 1985.

Slaughterhouse Cases, 16 Wall. (83 U.S.) 36, 21 L. Ed. 394 (1873).

Sparks, Jared, ed. *The Writings of George Washington.* Boston: Russell, Odiorne & Metcalf / Hilliard, Gray, 1834.

Stacey, Robert D. *Sir William Blackstone and the Common Law: Blackstone's Legacy to America.* Alliance Defense Fund Core Curriculum, ed. Jeffery J. Ventrella, no.1. Eugene, OR: ACW Press, 2003.

Tocqueville, Alexis de. *Democracy in America*, trans. and ed. Harvey C. Mansfield and Delba Winthrop. Chicago: University of Chicago Press, 2000.

Uhlmann, Michael M. "The Road Not Taken: *Brown v. Board of Education* at 50." *Claremont Review of Books* 4, No. 3 (Summer 2004).

Zacharias, Ravi. *Deliver Us from Evil: Restoring the Soul in a Disintegrating Culture.* Nashville: Thomas Nelson, 1998.